TESTS
that TEACH

Using Standardized Tests to Improve Instruction

Karen Tankersley

 Association for Supervision and Curriculum Development • Alexandria, Virginia USA

Association for Supervision and Curriculum Development
1703 N. Beauregard St. • Alexandria, VA 22311-1714 USA
Phone: 800-933-2723 or 703-578-9600 • Fax: 703-575-5400
Web site: www.ascd.org • E-mail: member@ascd.org
Author guidelines: www.ascd.org/write

Gene R. Carter, *Executive Director;* Nancy Modrak, *Director of Publishing;*
Julie Houtz, *Director of Book Editing & Production;* Deborah Siegel, *Project Manager;*
Georgia Park, *Senior Graphic Designer;* Valerie Younkin, *Desktop Publishing
Specialist;* Sarah Plumb, *Production Specialist*

All Web links in this book are correct as of the publication date below but may
have become inactive or otherwise modified since that time. If you notice a
deactivated or changed link, please e-mail books@ascd.org with the words "Link
Update" in the subject line. In your message, please specify the Web link, the book
title, and the page number on which the link appears.

PAPERBACK ISBN: 978-1-4166-0579-9 ASCD product #107022   s8/07
Also available as an e-book through ebrary, netLibrary, and many online
booksellers (see Books in Print for the ISBNs).

Quantity discounts for the paperback edition only: 10–49 copies, 10%; 50+ copies,
15%; for 1,000 or more copies, call 800-933-2723, ext. 5634, or 703-575-5634.
For desk copies: member@ascd.org.

Library of Congress Cataloging-in-Publication Data
Tankersley, Karen, 1952–
    Tests that teach : using standardized tests to improve instruction / Karen
Tankersley.
        p. cm.
    Includes bibliographical references and index.
    ISBN-13: 978-1-4166-0579-9 (pbk. : alk. paper) 1. Educational tests and
measurements—United States. 2. Effective teaching—United States. 3. Academic
achievement—United States. I. Title.
    LB3051.T26 2007
    371.26'2—dc22
                                                                2007016645

──

18 17 16 15 14 13 12 11 10 09 08 07   1 2 3 4 5 6 7 8 9 10 11 12

*This book is dedicated to
Emily and Mandi.*

*May your lives be filled
with health,
wealth, and happiness.*

TESTS THAT TEACH

Using Standardized Tests to Improve Instruction

Introduction

Over the past decade, many school districts have begun to use data to analyze the academic performance of the students they serve. Schools have used data on student performance to examine how well they compare to other schools as well as to track how students are performing over time. Administrators and teachers have used data to make critical decisions about what to do and when to do it.

Effective schools use a recursive cycle of assessment and critical analysis to examine the mountains of student performance data generated year after year. They regularly collect data about their students, examine school programs and practices, scrutinize and make meaning from the data, and even establish action plans to address concerns or problems arising from their study of the data. While this beneficial process has provided a strong foundation for focused school improvement efforts and should definitely be continued, school improvement efforts cannot stop here. Schools must also examine what happens in the classroom. The missing step that reflective schools must take is to carefully analyze state standards and to look at the way tasks and questions are structured and presented on state assessments. Just as it makes a difference what content students are asked about on state tests, it makes a difference how questions are asked and what tasks students are expected to perform. For most districts, this performance gap occurs on the constructed-response sections of their state assessments. When cognitive expectations of the classroom do not match assessment measures, a disconnect occurs between instruction and assessment performance. If teachers do not regularly ask students to synthesize their learning and apply their knowledge and skills in more sophisticated and unique ways, how can we expect students to suddenly be able to do so at assessment time? Even though schools are continually making efforts to enhance student performance, if daily instruction does not prepare students to easily respond to the constructed-response questions, students will continue to stumble on these sections of the test. What goes on in the classroom on a daily basis matters and matters greatly.

Although many state and national assessments contain multiple-choice test items, most states have also incorporated some "open-ended" or constructed-response test items into their own tests. Those that do not have them already designed into their testing instruments are currently planning revisions, so it is likely that all states will soon incorporate constructed-response items into their student performance assessments. Under the threat of losing federal funds, states are expanding not only the content areas tested but also the number of grade levels to be tested. Student accountability has also been increased in many states. As of the 2005–06 school year, at least 22 states have developed and are implementing a graduation test as a requirement for receiving a high school graduation diploma. Clearly, constructed-response items will not be going away any time soon, so teachers must learn how to design lessons that enable students to perform well on these types of assessments.

This disconnect between what students are expected to do on assessments and actual classroom instruction can be seen not only on state assessments but also on the National Assessment of Educational Progress (NAEP) test, which tracks national student performance in key content areas. When we examine national data, we can see that on the constructed-response items, student performance lags behind more traditional performance measures. At least half of the items contained on the NAEP test administered to a sampling of students across the nation are constructed-response items, which expect students to make inferences, explain, organize, analyze, and apply learning in much deeper ways. For these reasons, it is essential that teachers know how to use instructional practices that solidly prepare students to meet the demands that state tests will require of them.

The testing requirements and accountability measures facing schools and teachers today have been contested by various educational groups in the United States. Nevertheless, accountability pressures are not likely to be eased any time soon, so to debate whether students should or should not be tested is not a good use of our time. The fact remains that as long as testing remains a part of the way schools and teachers are measured, educators must know and understand the "rules" by which score is kept. For this reason, it is imperative that teachers learn to use instructional techniques that raise student expectations and learning to more intense levels of thinking and independence than ever before.

This book will help you develop the skills and understanding to teach beyond the rote facts and memorization stage and help your students truly apply the skills they are learning as independent and deep thinkers. You will be able to challenge and stretch young minds in more effective ways and ensure that assessment truly measures daily instruction. You will learn how to build a supportive, collaborative school environment where the entire staff works to clarify expectations and set consistent, achievable performance measures. By implementing strategies that allow students to build their skills, learn self-assessment, and provide a supportive and meaningful environment, you will be able to better prepare your students not only to score well on state and national assessments but to take their place as thoughtful and organized thinkers in a rapidly changing, competitive society.

1 Constructed Response: Connecting Performance and Assessment

Helping Students Prepare for the Future

Early in their school careers, students learn that the teacher has the "right" answers to questions asked in the classroom. Successful students learn that their "job" is to try to figure out that "right" answer and to provide it for the teacher. Students who are able to do this quickly and accurately are perceived as brighter and are rewarded with higher grades and more positive feedback. Students who have difficulty in perceiving the answer the teacher is seeking may well be viewed as less competent and are less tolerated. In far too many classrooms, teachers do not require students to think deeply or move beyond the basic knowledge and comprehension level. Even those students who are perceived as bright, capable learners are seldom asked questions like "How do you know?" or "How did you get that answer?" or "Why do you think so?" or "Show me proof that answer is correct." This lack of cognitive follow-through in our classrooms leads to shallow thinking and encourages students to simply try to guess what the teacher is thinking during instruction rather than really cognitively engage in deep thinking and learning.

Another issue that has limited the depth of thinking and learning in American classrooms is that our ever-expanding curriculum has been "a mile wide and an inch deep." Traditional classrooms have emphasized facts and rote information at the expense of requiring students to apply higher-order thinking activities. As knowledge in the world continues to explode at exponential levels, this is no longer practical. Instead, students must be able to manage information and apply the appropriate level of sophistication needed to think deeply and process complex problems.

To solve problems in real-world situations, students must be able to apply knowledge and use thinking strategies to analyze, synthesize, and evaluate information. In the real world, answers are seldom black and white, and there are often many solutions to a problem. Preparing students with only surface-level knowledge does not lead to "deep thinking," to intellectual independence, or to building a student's capacity to problem solve and analyze complex situations in the real world. Requiring students to think and process information at much deeper levels prepares them for the real role they will face in life and in tomorrow's workplace. We might be surprised at just how capable our students are if we push them to reach beyond where they are currently performing. As Mem Fox (1993) so aptly puts it in her book, *Radical Reflections*, "If we allow children to show us what they can do rather than accepting what they usually do, we would be in for some grand surprises. As adults, our feeble expectations of children's capabilities puts brakes on their potential" (p. 65).

Preparing students to think deeply, thoroughly, and critically is a task we cannot begin too early. If we create classrooms where students are willing to take risks, share their ideas and thoughts, delve deeply into issues and ideas, and take responsibility for their own learning, our students will become deep thinkers who will not only perform well today but also be more prepared for the increasingly complex world they will face tomorrow.

Public Accountability and High-Stakes Testing

Since the rise of the industrial era, one of the major roles of the public educational system has been to prepare students for the workplace. The public educational system, as it existed during much of the first half of the 20th century, was designed to prepare students to either continue on to college or to develop vocational skills that could be transferred upon graduation directly to the workplace. During the

1970s and 1980s, rapid breakthroughs in technology and increased pressures from global competition caused business leaders to begin questioning the preparedness of American graduates and the rigor of the curriculum of public school systems across the United States. Policymakers responded with passage of the Carl D. Perkins Vocational and Applied Technical Educational Act of 1984. As the economic noose continued to tighten around the profit margins of American companies, business and community leaders continued to pressure state and local policymakers for educational reform.

In 1994, President Clinton signed the $300 million School-to-Work Opportunities Act followed by the more aggressive Improving America's Schools Act of 1994 (Goals 2000) legislation. Goals 2000 funds ushered in the establishment of subject content standards by national professional organizations such as the International Reading Association and the National Council of Teachers of Math and other similar content organizations and movement toward uniform national curriculum standards. The Improving America's Schools Act of 1994 required states to adopt or develop their own state standards and to align assessments to grade-level benchmark standards. This act also required Title I schools to show progress on those assessments for continued funding allocations, which was a direct government attempt to control student performance via funding.

On the U.S. Department of Labor (DOL) Web site, one can find a table listing the 30 fastest-growing jobs from the 2006–07 Occupational Outlook Handbook. The table lists not only the number of jobs expected to be produced in coming years but also the level of education required to qualify for these occupations. Just six of these jobs can be obtained with "on the job training" only, while 80 percent of the remaining occupational titles will require postsecondary education. Of these 30 fast-growing careers, 30 percent will require an associate's degree, 33 percent will require a bachelor's degree, and 17 percent will require a master's or doctoral degree (U.S. DOL, 2007). National concern over ever-widening gaps in achievement and poverty status in ballooning minority populations has also surfaced. With mounting pressure for highly skilled, technically literate workers from business and political leaders, President George W. Bush formed a bipartisan coalition in 2000 to draft a more stringent version of national educational policy. This new policy, known as the No Child Left Behind Act (NCLB), established national goals that all children would reach proficiency in key content areas by 2012 and provided sanctions for failure to meet targeted goals and progress measures. Congress supported the plan, and the highly directive NCLB legislation overwhelmingly passed the House by a vote of 381–41 and the Senate by a vote of 87–10.

During the past couple of decades, business and community leaders have been loudly demanding that schools be held publicly accountable for student performance. This demand for accessible accountability is so apparent that an Internet search can provide information about the academic performance of any school in the country. The information is posted not only by the various state departments of education and often the school districts themselves but also by private organizations. These businesses make money by providing the public with various perceptual and performance statistics about schools anywhere in the country. We are also likely to hear how local school districts and schools have fared on state assessments on television, on the radio, and even on the front page of the newspaper in every city in the country. Everyone wants to know how their local schools have performed and expects to have easy access to this information as soon as it is available. The performance of local schools and school districts influences the price of real estate and where people buy their homes. It also determines whether voters are supportive of increased school funding needs in the local area.

Although education is a "state's right issue," even the federal government has taken steps to ensure more uniform accountability. As public accountability intensifies, pressure on state governments to ensure compliance has also magnified. Not only are test results being associated with specific school districts, but they are more increasingly viewed as a reflection of the instructional skills of the individual classroom teacher. Recent Federal Register grant offerings demonstrate that policymakers are encouraging states to move accountability measures (both rewards and sanctions) down to the individual teacher level. In many areas, "pay for performance" measures are increasingly the focus of new pay structures for teachers. School districts such as Denver and

Houston have already begun using student performance as the basis for teacher merit pay, and the movement is growing at both the state and federal levels. Despite the unpopularity of "pay for performance" with teacher labor groups, pay systems tied to student achievement are only likely to increase in the foreseeable future as researchers find ways to separate out the threads that link student growth directly to the instructional impact of a single teacher. Helping students perform well on state academic assessments is no longer optional but, rather, essential to a teacher's career and financial well-being. Whether we like it or not, high accountability, public scrutiny, and pressure for performance are here to stay.

The Standards Movement: What Should Students Know and Be Able to Do?

To better understand how we got here, let's take a look at the educational trends over that past few decades. With the high-tech industry exploding, business leaders and legislators were making public calls in the 1980s for raising student achievement, especially in the areas of reading, writing, and mathematics. Because educational expectations were different from state to state, demands to increase instructional rigor and develop national curricular standardization were loudly touted. National professional organizations saw the writing on the wall and responded by developing, with professionals from the field, their own sets of benchmark "standards" to delineate the key curriculum for their content areas. The standards movement and "standards-based instruction" were born.

As each professional curriculum group released their "standards" documents, state educational departments across the country took these guidelines and personalized them, subject by subject, to meet the needs of their own students. Copies of the state content standards were shipped to districts, and educators received their own state's versions of the "standards" delineating what students should know and be able to do. Often these early standard guidelines were broadly written and may even have spanned several grades with the same basic criteria for mastery. Although teachers' unions responded that the new standards limited teacher creativity and educational freedom, state departments were quick to assure local school districts that there was substantial room for "teacher interpretation" at the classroom level. Most states then pressed forward with developing new "standards-based assessments" for key "benchmark" grades in at least the core content areas of reading, writing, and mathematics to measure their new curriculum.

After the passage of NCLB, federal reporting requirements forced states to ramp up testing to more grade levels and more content areas, including science. State plans had to receive approval at the federal level, or the state would risk losing not only federal educational funds but all federal state aid as well. A few states considered opting out of the federal requirements or even filing a judicial challenge to the requirements, but soon all changed their positions and began working to meet the regulations of the law. Although states still varied widely in content expectations and academic rigor, one giant step toward a more uniform, standard curriculum and the measurement of student performance had been taken.

Second-Generation Assessments Require Deeper Thinking

Many of the first state assessment instruments contained primarily multiple-choice types of items. As testing instruments became more sophisticated, short-answer and open-ended, constructed-response items where students had to apply their knowledge on a more complex performance-oriented task began to appear more frequently. As states continue to make revisions, more and more constructed-response questions are being incorporated into assessment instruments.

If we examine the content standards now in place in most states, we will see that they require students to use higher-order thinking and reasoning skills rather than just memorize content information. This emphasis on higher-order thinking reflects the philosophy that while content knowledge and basic skills are important, it is the ability to reason and apply those skills that truly demonstrates mastery of content.

Despite the fact that the tests have changed to include a greater emphasis on higher-order thinking with performance-based measures, some teachers have not changed the way they approach their daily instruction. For this reason, it is in the constructed-response sections where students are having difficulty applying their knowledge. This results in lower overall scores on these parts of the state test. With changes to how we approach daily instruction, we can help our students develop the skills they need not only to do well on these assessment items but also to internalize what we are trying to teach them.

It is beyond the scope of this book to debate the merits or pitfalls of high-stakes testing. If one is interested in reading about this debate, a plethora of information on this issue is available on the Internet. Regardless of whether we feel high-stakes testing is good or bad, it exists, and until the political realities change, these are the "rules" under which we must operate. Like it or not, accountability is reality. For me, it is a waste of time to debate what I cannot control. I have chosen to take the path of helping teachers understand how to provide their students with the best possible preparation for success on state assessments, since this student success is critical.

This book will help teachers understand how to teach on a daily basis so that students can easily rise to the challenge of scoring well on state assessments, particularly on the constructed-response sections of these instruments. Your students' success is your success. This book will help you understand how to create a classroom that supports deep thinking and higher-order performance so that your students have the best chance to show what they know and are able to do.

What Is Constructed Response?

Let's start with a definition of what constructed-response items are so we have a common understanding of what the term means. *Constructed-response questions* are assessment items that ask students to apply knowledge, skills, and critical thinking abilities to real-world, standards-driven performance tasks. Sometimes called "open-response" items, constructed-response questions are so named because there is often more than one way to correctly answer the question, and they require students to "construct" or develop their own answers without the benefit of any suggestions or choices.

Constructed-response items can be very simple, requiring students to answer with only a sentence or two, or quite complex, requiring students to read a prompt or a specified text article, reflect on the key points, and then develop a meaningful essay or analysis of the information. Whether simple or complex, all constructed-response questions measure students' ability to apply, analyze, evaluate, and synthesize the knowledge that they have acquired in a more abstract way.

Although most states primarily use open-ended response questions on their state assessment instruments, some use constructed-response questions in a "closed" format. Closed constructed-response questions are similar to more traditional fill-in-the-blank types of questions and have only one right answer. They ask students to fill in a word or a phrase in a specific text and usually require only simple recall or, at best, an inference. Here's an example of a closed type of question: "According to the passage, Allen did not want _____ to go with the group to the park." Although students might have to make an inference from the text passage, there is still only one correct answer that can complete the question, so divergent thinking or unique responses are unnecessary. Despite the fact that making an inference is considered a higher-order skill, the question still merely requires students to identify the correct answer. Closed questions generally do not stretch a student's thinking to any great extent.

In contrast, open-ended questions require students to think deeply about the question and to provide a much more in-depth response. Here's an example of such a question: "The principal thinks students need more time for learning and wants to do away with recess for all grades at your school. Write a persuasive essay telling him why you either agree or disagree with this idea." This type of question requires students to think about a specific issue, evaluate their position on it, and then organize their thoughts and compose a meaningful, persuasive essay on the topic. This is a complex, high-level task that can demonstrate what the student knows and is independently able to do.

As we have already discussed, constructed-response questions may be simple or complex in nature, as in the example just given.

Here's an example of a simple prompt, commonly referred to as a "brief response" question: "Briefly tell why Mary was afraid in the story." Test makers might be looking for a student response such as "Mary was afraid because it was dark, and she has lost her key to get into her house. No one was home to let her in when she got home." Students who could identify losing the key and being locked out as two main concepts causing Mary to be afraid would likely be awarded the complete point allowance for the response. A student who simply noted that "It was dark" might be awarded only a portion of the possible response points because although one piece of the answer was correct, the response was missing other key details that were also required for full points. In this response, the student did not demonstrate a thorough understanding of the fact that Mary's loss of the key was the event that caused her to be locked out in the dark.

Sometimes test makers provide a specific stimulus for students to use in constructing a response. Students may be presented with a graphic organizer, a map, a picture, or a diary excerpt that they must use as background information for the task they are asked to do. They may be asked to process the information, make inferences, or analyze information based on this stimulus. Students are then expected to write anything from a sentence to a fully developed essay using the information presented and the connections and interpretations they have made. For example, in language arts, students may be asked to identify and cite examples from a short story to highlight changes in attitude that occur in the lead character from the beginning to the end of the story. In math, students may be asked to draw a diagram, interpret data, or develop a sequential solution that solves a specific problem. In social studies, they may be asked to discuss the meaning of a theme such as "nationalism" or to create a graphic organizer comparing two regions or two contrasting concepts such as communism and capitalism.

Alternatively, sometimes students must use information to create a graphic organizer, create and correctly label a diagram, or draw a diagram showing a solution. Complex constructed-response questions require substantially more response time and require that students have an understanding of the processes that will be needed to complete the task. More often than not, in a complex response, students will be asked to provide examples or illustrations or to justify their thinking on a particular topic. When text passages are used as the stimulus for the response, students are often asked to refer directly to the text to show connections or examples of the points they are trying to make. When students regularly practice justifying their thoughts and linking information back to their own ideas, their ability to do the same at assessment time increases substantially.

Constructed-response questions are generally criterion referenced and may measure one broad content standard or several specific content standards. Test items will usually be scored manually against a pre-established rubric and sets of prescored sample papers, called *anchor papers*, that identify the range of allowable responses for each score level. The anchor papers help raters establish a degree of uniformity in how each paper is scored on the established rubric. Scoring is holistic and relatively objective, based on the actual components included in the response. Students may receive full credit or partial credit based on the pre-established rubric criteria.

Scoring Constructed-Response Questions

Almost every state now incorporates constructed-response items into its state grade-level assessment instruments or graduation exams. While multiple-choice test items typically only carry 1 point per item, constructed-response items can account for as few as 2 points or as many as 10 points of the total raw score for each question. Depending on the state, constructed-response items may account for as much as 25 to 50 percent of the composition of the total test that students will be facing each year.

Not only are constructed-response questions more demanding, but their placement in the test booklet can add an additional challenge. Although these questions require more intense effort and processing power, most test writers put them at the end of the multiple-choice test segments. Because students may already be beginning to tire when they reach this point on the assessment, some have a tendency to gloss over the very items that require their most concentrated and deliberate efforts. As a result, some students lose points simply because they are too tired to devote the energy needed to complete the task. Each question is scored against a pre-established rubric, with partial credit being awarded for answers that may have some accuracy but are less fully developed. Unlike a multiple-choice question, which is scored either right or wrong, a constructed-response question can earn students partial credit for having some degree of accuracy in their response. In any case, with a constructed-response question, students have multiple options for organizing, processing the information, and creating a response that derives from their own thoughts, skills, and experiences. Helping students improve their ability to provide high-quality responses on the constructed-response test items can significantly improve students' scores because each constructed-response item may hold many points that could affect the overall score.

Teachers who routinely teach for deep understanding find that their students are also more motivated, interested, and involved in the learning process. Despite the increased use of constructed-response items on state and national assessments, many teachers have not changed their instructional approaches to help students practice responding in more comprehensive, open-ended ways. Deep thinking and processing must become the rule rather than the exception. While building superficial knowledge may have worked when tests were written entirely in a multiple-choice format, it is not enough now. We have seen that students lose the most points on the constructed-response sections, so clearly we must change how we work with students every day. Our daily instruction must help students delve deeper and go beyond the superficial knowledge. By understanding and incorporating open-ended activities into the regular instructional program, teachers can feel confident that their students will quickly become better prepared for meeting the challenges they will face on the constructed-response sections of assessments.

Classroom Instruction That Builds Thinking

Good teachers have always known that effective learning requires practice and very specific performance feedback to build success. Consider when a child learns to ride a two-wheeled bicycle for the first time. We provide support such as training wheels or more physical support such as holding onto the bike and running alongside the child until the child can balance the bicycle unaided. All during the process, we provide feedback or suggestions on how to combine the actions of balancing and pedaling at the same time. In addition to teaching the child how to move forward, we also describe how to stop, turn, and use appropriate safety procedures. At first the task is difficult, but with persistence, the child makes progress. Although he or she may still fall or be wobbly now and then, it is the continued practice and our coaching that eventually help the child learn to synthesize all of the information into accomplishing the task.

Constructed-response test questions entail a similar sequential process. For example, consider the following test item that might appear on a high school reading assessment: "Identify the mood in the passage from Joseph Conrad's novel *The Heart of Darkness*. Use at least four specific examples and details from the text to support your answer." This question would require students to read the given passage with sufficient comprehension not only to understand the concept of "mood" but also to analyze the text, choose relevant examples, and then support a logical argument about the text in written form. This is a complex task that many high school students find not only challenging but perhaps even overwhelming. It is therefore not surprising that students perform less well on open-ended, constructed-response items on state and national assessments than they do on multiple-choice items. At least with a multiple-choice item, depending on the number of responses presented for each question, students have a one-in-four or perhaps a one-in-five chance of answering correctly, even when they have no idea what the right answer may be. Constructed-response questions, in contrast, require students to supply their own answer to the question, commonly referred to as a "prompt."

In reading or social studies, a multiparagraph passage can provide test developers with multiple questions that build from simple to complex. After reading the passage, students may be provided with a comprehensive prompt or a series of smaller response prompts all based on the same text. Here are examples of comprehensive prompts:

• "Write a paragraph summarizing the story."
• "What do you think was the lesson that Character X learned in this story?"
• "Choose someone that you know who is like Character X. List and discuss the ways this person is like Character X. Use examples and illustrations from the text to support your response."
• "Suggest a different ending to this story."

In other cases, students may need to create a chart showing the differences or simply draw conclusions and formulate an answer to a question. Questions might be written as follows: "What conclusions can you draw about population growth in Country X from the data presented in the chart?" or "Given the location of this country on the map shown, what issues or concerns would you expect the people who live in this country to have?" To respond successfully to these types of responses, students must be able to analyze the information and then be able to draw conclusions about the data. Sometimes the same data are used with brief-answer questions, all based on the same data set. In each case, students must reflect on the text to answer each of the open-ended questions in a thorough and comprehensive way.

In many states, the assessment of terminology and vocabulary is an integral part of state assessment instruments. To assess vocabulary knowledge, test makers frequently give students a short passage containing the target word and then ask them to interpret the meaning of a vocabulary term by selecting a multiple-choice sentence that correctly explains the usage of the word. Although these items are often multiple choice, they still require that students have a well-developed vocabulary to identify the correct response. Teachers can help students improve in this area by ensuring that students have a good understanding of how to use context clues and prefixes, suffixes, and root words to determine the probable meaning of a given word.

In some states, students are expected to be able to classify text by genre. Students might be asked not only to identify the genre but also to cite clues or information that helps categorize the text into this genre. Genre questions require that students fully understand the characteristics of various genres and are able to identify the elements that meet these characteristics in the passage. Here's an example of a genre question: "Discuss the elements found in this story that make it a fairy tale, and cite relevant examples from the story." If students have not been taught to identify the characteristics of various literary genres (and state standards expect them to do so), they will not be able to perform well on a constructed-response item of this type.

In math, open-ended questions are generally developed around one of the following five key areas: number sense and operations; patterns, relationships, and algebraic concepts; geometry; measurement; or data, statistics, and probability. Students may be asked to describe the steps taken to solve a particular problem, predict a sequence or pattern, or calculate specific values from a given chart or table. In many cases, students need to understand not only how to perform the necessary calculations but also how to sift through irrelevant data to find the essential pieces of information. Many states will also expect students to explain how they arrived at answers or to sequentially describe the steps they used to solve the problem. Students will also have to understand essential math terms and vocabulary such as *perimeter* and *area* that might appear in the problem, as well as be able to apply the appropriate skills correctly.

On science assessments, test makers may ask students to interpret data from maps of various types in order to draw conclusions or make predictions. They may also ask them to describe or draw various scientific components, such as the layers of soil or the atmosphere, or discuss how certain features help specific animals survive in their habitats or how certain cycles occur in nature. If students do not have a true understanding of the processes involved in these scientific elements, they will not be able to perform the tasks. Again, familiarizing yourself with the grade-level content standards and all state-released items will help you clearly understand the expectations set for your students.

Just as practice and feedback help a child learn to ride a bicycle, if we want students to score well on constructed-response items on their annual assessments, we must provide them with many opportunities to use higher-level thinking where we can coach and shape their abilities. Students need to be trained in how to analyze the requirements of a task, explain their thinking, and support their analysis or opinions with concrete evidence. We must ask them regularly to make connections, synthesize responses, analyze sets of data, and use all of their background knowledge to interpret information. When this activity has become the norm rather than the exception, then we will have truly accomplished our goal of preparing our students for the demands facing them.

Creating a Classroom Conducive to Higher Levels of Thinking

Classrooms that maximize student learning potential are environments where independent thinking is valued and students are encouraged to see themselves as capable problem solvers. The teacher's role becomes the "guide by the side" rather than the "sage on the stage." The atmosphere is supportive and nonthreatening so that risk taking and divergent thinking are encouraged and promoted. Questions are not answered primarily by the teacher but, rather, by the students themselves. Students are encouraged to experiment and grapple with ideas to make their own connections and find their own solutions. They are asked to explain their conclusions, outline their thought processes, and justify their decision making. In these classrooms, it is important to talk more about the process used to arrive at a specific response rather than about whether the answer was correct. In short, it is what the student has learned rather than what the teacher has taught that becomes the focus of daily operations.

To clarify this idea by again comparing it to performing a simple sport, we can conceptually teach a child to hold a baseball bat and to swing it at an oncoming ball. We can help the child understand the rules of baseball and even how to run from base to base or the points to consider for stealing a base, but we cannot teach that player how to apply all of these skills to maximize the chance of success. It is the player who must learn to evaluate, to strategize, and to combine all of these skills to play the game successfully. The degree to which each individual can successfully combine all of this training and information into successfully playing the game determines whether that person becomes an occasional player at the local park or a highly paid, major league professional. Likewise, how well students integrate what they have learned and practiced in the classroom helps determine their performance on assessments.

In classrooms that promote deep thinking, students receive ample time to explore and reflect on multiple perspectives. In these classrooms, learning is a community activity. Students frequently work together to develop, clarify, or blend their thoughts and ideas on the topics they are learning. They ask not only their teacher but one another for information, explanations, and clarifications on a regular basis. Activities draw from real-life examples that provide immediate and meaningful relevance to students' lives and experiences. Students understand that there may be more than one right answer and that process is just as important as an answer. They use a variety of communication tools such as drawings, diagrams, tables, and other forms of graphic organizers or visual displays to process and present their thoughts and ideas. Comparing, interpreting, and analyzing information become common tasks that permeate learning in the classroom.

As a classroom teacher, I always thought that the best learning occurred when I remembered that learning should, above all, be enjoyable and stimulating. The chapters that follow will help you enhance what has been successful for you as well as take your instructional practices to the next level. With these changes, your classroom can foster the kind of successful, complex, independent thinkers capable of facing the challenges of the 21st century.

2 | Classrooms That Create Deep Thinkers

Learning is like rowing upstream: not to advance is to drop back.

Chinese Proverb

Learning Is a Process

Understanding what students are expected to know and be able to do is the first step in designing activities that foster high student achievement. As discussed in the last chapter, effective teachers take time before they teach anything to their students to determine how they will know when students understand the skills and concepts they have been presented. In *Understanding by Design*, Wiggins and McTighe (1998) refer to this planning process as "backward design." In the backward design model, the teacher determines what students should know and be able to do, determines the gap between existing performance and target performance, and only then begins the instructional planning process. Once the performance gap has been determined, the teacher plans appropriate activities to build student skills and enable students to meet desired expectations. Assessments given at the conclusion of the activity verify student growth and begin the instructional cycle again.

Exactly what are students required to know and do to demonstrate learning in your state in each content area? Studying the state standards and any curricular material put out by your state or school district will help you determine what students are expected to know and be able to do at your particular grade level. For example, a language arts teacher might ask the following questions:

- What reading skills are students expected to master?
- What types of text should students practice reading?
- What terms should they know?
- What genres or text characteristics are students expected to know?
- What special literary terms should students in my grade level understand? (Examples of literary terms or concepts might be *plot, setting, theme, mood,* or *tone* or the concepts of foreshadowing or personification in text.)
- Do they know how to determine a main idea and identify supporting details?
- Should they be able to make an inference or draw a conclusion from text?
- What writing formats will students be required to know and be able to use—narrative, comparative, descriptive, poetic, expository, persuasive?
- What products are students expected to be able to produce—diary, memo, e-mail, letter, opinion paper, research paper, essay?

Study not only the standards related to your specific grade level but the standards of the grades immediately before and after your grade level to get a better feel for the level of mastery that is required of your students. What should students already know when you get them? What will they be expected to know before going to the next grade level? This list will be the core of what you present in various formats throughout the year. Be sure that you have thoroughly examined the information for your content area and that you have asked yourself the key questions for your content topic. When we are very clear about what it is students are responsible to know and be able to do, we can focus our energies on ensuring that these skills are embedded in daily instruction.

Once we know what our students are expected to master, we then need to have a good understanding of the skills that each student brings to our door. Specifically, before we can design any instruction, we must first determine what gaps lie between the skills they bring and the skills they are expected to master. This means pre-assessing our students' skills so that we clearly understand what they know and are able to do with regard to each skill and concept on our list. This cycle of assess-plan-teach-reassess is the basic foundation of how we must approach the small window of time we have with our students during the course of the school year.

Although this approach helps us plan our instructional year and make the most of that time, one other consideration is critical if we hope to maximize student performance on state assessments: what skills and understandings are students expected to demonstrate on state assessments? As noted in the previous chapter, most state tests consist of multiple-choice test items as well as more complex constructed-response items. While many students can select the correct response from a limited set of multiple-choice options, many of them struggle when it comes to actually creating their own responses with no assistance. Formulating a response requires a deep level of understanding and the appropriate skills to organize and construct an independent answer. As a result, we need to study the performance items in great detail. Understanding how students will be assessed in your content area is crucial to building the foundation for high-level student performance.

The first step toward understanding how to change instruction to match what students will be asked to do at assessment time is understanding exactly what is required of your students. Almost all states have either sample question booklets or a bank of old test questions, often referred to as "released items," available for teachers to study. Appendix A lists links to state department Web sites where you can learn what information might be available on your own state's testing program. You might also want to contact your district curriculum or testing coordinator to see if any additional sources of information are available to help teachers understand state standards and assessment requirements. Appendix A also contains links to many other state and private sources where you can find examples of lesson plans, test-taking tips, and even predesigned assessments that you can download and use in your own classroom. Take the time to thoroughly study and dissect all materials available to you regarding your own state assessments, as well as any available materials from states that use evaluation formats similar to those of your own state. When you clearly understand what students are expected to know and be able to do, you can provide students frequent opportunities to regularly process your content in similar ways.

Let's consider some examples of tasks that students might face on typical state content-area constructed-response questions. In language arts, for example, constructed-response activities are usually developed around a text passage. Sometimes this passage is a story or a section of a play, but it could also be a poem or an excerpt from a nonfiction article that students have been given to read. Questions often focus on identifying the five kinds of text elements: the main idea or the author's approach, supporting details, relationships (sequential, comparative, or cause and effect), the meaning of various vocabulary words, and generalizations and conclusions. Chapter 3 will provide a more detailed look at helping students excel on typical language arts state assessment instruments.

Because of the No Child Left Behind requirement that students be tested in science in addition to other core content areas, many states are in the process of either developing or radically revising their state assessments in science. If we examine the online sample assessments from even just a handful of states, it is easy to see that assessments in these areas vary greatly in the amount of content covered and the expectations for performance that the state has set for students in either area. One of the most obvious sources for constructed-response questions in science is the experiment. Science assessments typically ask students about systems, processes, cause-and-effect relationships, and connections between these things. Chapter 4 will provide an analysis of the current state of science assessment and how teachers can assist students in this content area.

Social studies, while not yet mandated at the federal level, is tested in some states but not in others. Social studies tests vary widely from state to state and may assess students on everything from U.S. history to world history, to civics or citizenship, to geography or even economics. This is a tall order unless social studies teachers clearly understand what students are expected to know and be able to do.

Most state assessments in social studies are based on short text passages, statements about historical events, maps, charts, diagrams, political cartoons, slogans, posters of the era, or even pictures of a certain time period. In states such as New York, students are expected to read, interpret, and respond to questions using original historical documents as well as all of the items just listed. For New York 8th grade students, multiple-choice questions make up only 50 percent of the state social studies assessment. The other half of the test that students will face is clearly higher level in construction. Constructed-response questions make up an additional 20 percent of the state assessment, with document-based questions making up the final 30 percent. For New York students, having experience reading and interpreting various historical documents is critical to success. We will explore strategies to help teachers successfully prepare students for various types of social studies assessments in Chapter 5.

Constructed-response questions in math are often designed around a text "situation" or "problem" that students must solve using various mathematical procedures. Other constructed-response math questions ask the student to read or interpret information from a picture, graph, or chart of some type. The student may also be expected to sort between relevant and irrelevant data or perform several mathematical steps or manipulations to arrive at a solution to the problem. In longer and more complex activities, the student may be presented with a problem as well as charts or graphs that must be correctly interpreted to develop an appropriate response. Chapter 6 will provide many ideas on ways to better prepare students in the area of math.

Teaching for Deeper Levels of Understanding

Prior to the standards era, most teachers organized their lesson content around whatever scope and sequence charts and textbooks they had been given. While this approach was effective during this time period, it is no longer sufficient. Standards-based teaching requires teachers to use a more "diagnostic-prescriptive" approach to lesson planning. As information explodes exponentially, we can no longer concentrate on imparting knowledge and facts to our students. We must help students understand how to locate information when needed, sift out the key understandings that are required, and then apply that information to develop solutions to the problems they face in their world. That is what preparing students to think deeply is all about.

We must analyze the gap between what students need to be able to do and what they can do at the present time. Precise, diagnostic lesson planning involves identifying what students will be able to do after your instruction that they could not do before. Effective teachers with high-performing students plan their instruction by identifying exactly what they want their students to be able to do as a result of instruction. They analyze current student performance levels and determine objectives needed to move students to the next performance level as well as the sequence in which those objectives should be presented. They design experiences that will build the needed skills while at the same time allowing students some degree of independence and responsibility for their own learning. Effective teachers organize instruction into small increments and regularly coach their students and model along the way. They create assessments and scoring rubrics that will help them measure student progress. In addition to providing their own feedback to students on how to improve performance, they also teach students how to self-assess and adjust their own performance. Students can hit the targets set for them because they clearly understand what "excellent" looks like. As students become active participants in their own learning, they develop into thinking, purposeful learners who can easily apply their understandings to new problems and situations.

Designing Lessons That Reinforce Higher-Order Thinking

As we discussed earlier, if we want students to score well on state assessments, we have to first identify what students must be able to accomplish. For example, on a state assessment in language arts, my students might need to read two poems; identify the theme and mood of each poem; be able to determine the meaning of several key words in context; and then write a detailed essay comparing the authors' writing styles in the two poems, using examples and details to illustrate the key points of the essay. On a math assessment, students might be asked to read background information on a problem, sift through both relevant and irrelevant information, select and apply an appropriate algorithm, set up at least one equation (if not a multistep problem), sequentially solve that equation, and then write about the process and how the problem was solved. Clearly, this is a tall order for even our bright students, much less the students who come to us with poor skills, weak background knowledge, or second language issues. It's no wonder we often feel overwhelmed by the demands placed on our students for content performance.

Going back to our hypothetical language arts example, if we know that students will be expected to use poems in the manner described in the last paragraph, we must ask students to read lots of poems and do the same type of analysis on a regular basis throughout the school year if we hope to have them do this task on a state assessment.

On state science assessments, if my students are expected to critique science experiments, then my lessons should center around helping students understand how to conduct a high-quality experiment by actually participating in experiments themselves. Students can't critique or identify errors in a process that is unfamiliar to them. Olympic sprinters do not begin running just before the Olympic Games if they expect to have any hope of doing well. They start years before the big event and practice constantly, with a coach by their side to refine their skills. At the risk of sounding pedantic, test preparation does not just suddenly begin once winter break is over and assessment time is looming. If I want my students to truly be able to show what they know and can do, test prep begins on day one of the school year and continues throughout the year.

To get yourself organized, begin by listing the tasks and understandings in your chosen content area that are difficult for students. Here are some questions to ask yourself:

• What are the things that give them trouble and that I will need to specifically teach?
• What will they be expected to use to create their responses?

- What stimulus items will students typically see on state assessments—charts, graphs, text, pictures, historical documents, concept-dense material?
- What vocabulary will they be expected to know?
- What problems will students have in processing the material or the understandings that will be necessary?
- What can I do to better prepare them to understand or front-load their foundational skills?
- What are essential understandings or skills that they must master in the content area no matter what their ability level?

Identify the key issues and stumbling blocks that might prevent your students from doing as well as you would like them to do. Plan ways to build student skills and address the concerns that you know will impede learning. Take time at the beginning of the year to lay a solid foundation under students so you can continue to build on this foundation for the rest of the school year.

As stated in Chapter 1, we know from testing data that students do relatively well on the multiple-choice questions but not as well on the open-ended, constructed-response types of questions on our state assessments. Ripple and Drinkwater (1982), in their review of research on the transfer of learning, say, "The concept of learning-to-learn implies the development of strategies or learning sets as a result of such experience (practice with a variety of problems). Preliminary practice on tasks that will transfer positively to performance on different criterion tasks is required for the development of learning to learn strategies" (p. 1949). Based on this finding, it is necessary for students to have experiences similar to what they will be expected to produce on state assessment tasks if we hope to ensure their success. Go through your state standards as well as any "released items" provided, and make a list to answer the following two questions:

- What must students be able to do in order to successfully produce the kinds of responses they will need?
- What instructional processes will prepare my students with the depth of knowledge they will need to think critically and produce the highest-quality responses possible?

Jot down the types of stimulus items that they are likely to see as well. We can model this process by helping our students use and analyze the same types of source stimulus as those used on the state exam. For example, if students are expected to examine a historical document and draw conclusions about it, then be sure they have frequent opportunities to do just that. If students are expected to read data on complex charts and then draw mathematical conclusions, again, make sure that they have regular opportunities to do just that. Being able to practice with similar stimuli and similar tasks will help students think beyond mere facts and information.

Planning Targeted Instruction for Constructed Response

In many content areas, students will answer broad questions that blend their background knowledge, their ability to think and process information, and perhaps some information specifically provided to them in a text passage. We often refer to these as "global" questions because they require a broad and comprehensive or "global" approach. Global questions are used in all content areas, so teachers must understand how to help students respond to them.

To answer global questions, students first need to be able to quickly scan a text for specific information they will need. Second, they must be able to understand and summarize the overall gist of the passage. Questions on a state assessment might be the following:

Elementary: "After reading the article, name at least one difference and one similarity between wolves and coyotes."

Secondary: "After reading the article, what advice would the reader conclude that the author is most trying to give parents?"

In the first example, students need to be able to read and understand the points being made in the text and then classify information based on similarities and differences. The needed skills for this task are comprehension and identifying similarities and differences. In the second example, students must read and understand the text's key points and also be able to summarize the gist of those key points. In this case, the students may have to make inferences and draw conclusions as well as clearly state the article's main idea. In both cases, students are asked to think deeply and apply a specific set of skills to the task.

As a result, the skills students will need must be modeled and specifically taught in the classroom. For example, a common component of state testing items is to require students to "use examples and details" from the story to support a response. Completing this task in an acceptable way requires that students understand the passage, be able to return to the text to scan for specific information, and then incorporate this information correctly into a constructed response. Again, these are specific skills that must be taught to students if you expect them to become proficient.

Here is a procedure that we might use to help our students learn to scan text and incorporate text into a response: Make a transparency of a short article from a newspaper, magazine, or the Internet, so that you can use this text to model the process for your students. Begin by teaching your students to identify and write down a question that is to be answered from the article title or a boldfaced heading within the article that seems important. This will help them link reading the text with answering a specific question. In our earlier example of a secondary prompt, students were asked to summarize the advice that the author gave to parents. For this article, we might write down, "What advice is the author giving to parents?" Writing down the question before scanning the text helps students focus specifically on what it is they are seeking. This process also releases the mind to now concentrate and process the text. Next, we need to make our thinking apparent to students by "thinking aloud" as we are processing the text. Here's the basic procedure for the think-aloud approach:

1. Orally describe your thinking for students as you quickly scan the text for specific clue words that might answer the question. Slow down the process so that students can hear how you process words and sentences and make decisions about the text. Say exactly what you are thinking as you read through the article so that students can hear how you reflect on the information.

2. Help them "listen in" on your thoughts. The most important part of the process for some students, particularly struggling students, is

being able to hear the modeling of a "successful thinker" performing a reading task.

3. As you find appropriate material in the text, demonstrate high-lighting or underlining the material that seems like it might possibly answer the question that has been written. Model jotting down some notes to help answer the question on a nearby whiteboard or chalk-board if possible.

4. Once you have demonstrated how to locate information that helps answer the question, demonstrate in the same oral manner how to compose a paragraph to respond to the question and summarize the information.

5. Model how to incorporate quotations or citations within the paragraph as you construct your response with students watching.

After students have watched you model a "talk-through" with a pas-sage, allow them to practice developing and answering questions in pairs with a different article. In the beginning, have students also talk through their thinking with a partner. Continue to practice orally until students can easily list the passage's key points. After they can do this well, have them add writing an appropriate response by including details and illustrations. Again, be sure you preface all instruction by modeling exactly what you want students to do by themselves.

After you have presented the strategy and had students directly practice it, begin to incorporate this same type of questioning into your daily instruction. Continue to ask students questions like these:

- "What are three reasons that. . . ?"
- "What three things do X and Y have in common?"
- "Do you think that. . . ? Why?"
- "How do you know?"
- "What makes you say that?"
- "Show me in the text why you think that."
- "What proof can you show me to support that?"

Require students to provide "evidence" by citing the page and para-graph from the text that support their response. I call this "prove it to me" support. Justifying answers helps ensure that students really are processing deeply, not just tossing out answers in the hopes of snagging the right one in passing. When students cite their rationale and the sources that led to their ideas and conclusions, you can observe how they are thinking. This enables you to catch misunderstandings and gaps in comprehension as they occur. Using think-aloud techniques paired with deliberate practice and feedback will build strong literal as well as inferential skills. It will also enable students to comfortably scan material for relevant information in all content areas.

Designing Instruction That Stretches Students' Minds

To learn something in a meaningful way, we must be able to relate our own personal background knowledge to the new information. Information crammed into a mind without any understanding of how it connects to or interacts with other information one already knows is useless. When learning is not linked to prior knowledge, the brain doesn't know how to store it or how to categorize it within memory. Think about the last thing you tried to learn that was very difficult for you. When learning is difficult, we feel frustrated, often feeling that the information just isn't "connecting" or making sense to us. This is because we have no background knowledge with which to link the information, so it remains elusive. Information that is not fully understood is not usable to us. We cannot connect it to anything else we may already know, nor can we apply it in any new situation. Information that doesn't make sense to us never makes it into our long-term memory. This is what happens when we "cram" facts or information that has little meaning to us for a one-shot test. Although we may be able to ace the test, we will quickly forget the information. In this case, learning is only superficial. For learning to be accessible and long-lasting, it must be meaningful and connected to other things we know. In other words, we must be able to create a web of connections around the particular information or learning.

Two other tools help students build good foundational skills in any content area, and all content teachers should incorporate them into daily instruction. The first is the use of visual displays and graphic organizers to sort, label, categorize, identify, and interconnect information. Many students learn best by visual means, so linking instruction with visual elements—in addition to tactile and aural elements—helps more students learn. Hundreds of books and Web resources suggest various designs for charts, graphs, and other sorts of web displays that will work well in your content area. These resources help students think critically and compartmentalize information for better recall. Graphic organizers require active thinking and help students reconstruct information in their own words. Processing text in this way helps students build ownership of ideas and helps teachers catch misconceptions or incorrect connections that a student might be making. Find as many types of graphic organizers as possible that will help students organize your content information more effectively.

Another instructional strategy that can help students deepen their understandings of text is the ability to identify similarities and differences. According to Marzano, Pickering, and Pollock (in the book *Classroom Instruction That Works* 2001), "researchers have found these mental operations to be basic to human thought. Indeed, they might be considered the 'core' of all learning" (p. 14). Questions that require that students make comparisons between concepts, characters, procedures, systems, or some other facet of a content area are some of the most commonly found types of constructed-response items. Finding similarities as well as differences in any content area requires deep thinking and clear understandings of the material being presented. Teachers in all content areas should help students learn to compare and contrast all aspects of their topic at every opportunity. Marzano and his colleagues further advise that while teachers may wish to provide direct instruction when focusing on specific similarities and differences, "if the teacher's goal is to stimulate divergence in students' thinking, however, then he should provide students with a student-directed activity" (p. 16). This can be done by having students define similarities and differences on graphic organizers, create metaphors or analogies to demonstrate their understandings, or write about their thinking in a reflective essay format. The more students can connect similarities and differences with concepts they already know, the more solidly new concepts and information can be linked to what has already been processed and stored in the brain.

Once we have identified the task, the skills to be learned, and how we will prepare our students to learn the necessary skills, we need to outline the steps that our students will take to complete the tasks. The more real or "authentic" the task, the more students will care about completing it to the best of their ability. Again, think about the tasks your students will be asked to perform on assessments, and create as many similar opportunities for them to practice as possible. If students are asked to write letters at assessment time, then find ways to write letters that are appropriate, relevant, and about topics of interest to your students. When students are given tasks they care about, their interest and motivation go up dramatically.

In the days of the Industrial Revolution, when people were being groomed for repetitious, solitary jobs on the assembly line, it was helpful to encourage students to work on tasks by themselves. Now, we work in collaborative teams in the workplace and share responsibilities with others for the success or failure of our tasks and projects. We should help our students support one another and learn to complete tasks as a collaborative team. Allowing students to complete tasks as partners or in small groups of three or four can provide the support that students need to be more successful. The goal is for each student to develop understandings that go deep enough that they can be applied, analyzed, synthesized, evaluated, and turned inside out. When this happens, true learning that can last a lifetime takes place.

Teaching Students to Use Rubrics to Analyze Their Own Performance

We often talk about the "teachable moment"—that moment when the conditions are just right to be able to impart learning to our students. Just as there are special times when we can influence our students in meaningful and relevant ways, there are times in our own careers when we also experience a "teachable moment." Someone—often one of our students—says or does something that helps us reflect on our own teaching philosophies or practices. When the teachable moment happens to a teacher, we gain a deeper understanding of our craft and usually a new way of approaching teaching.

In my second year of teaching, one such teachable moment occurred to me when a very bright high school student asked me to explain why teachers used tests. When I replied that teachers used tests to find out what students know and don't know, he informed me that he disagreed. He thought many teachers used tests simply to trick students and to play "gotcha" games with them. I asked why he believed that. He told me that from his viewpoint, some teachers tried to find the most obscure things in the textbook or lecture to place on the test so that students would be sure to miss the item. I started to disagree, of course, but he looked me in the eye and said, "If teachers really want to know what kids understand, then they should tell them what is important and then not try to trick them on their tests." While on the surface this may seem like a benign conversation, I thought a lot about his point that tests should measure what kids are supposed to know and not what is unimportant or trivial. That lesson has stayed with me and changed my teaching philosophies. Grading and testing should not be secrets and should never be attempts to "trick" or "confuse" students. I have come to agree with this young man that teachers should make it clear to their students what is important and what they are responsible for knowing. Share how you will grade students on their work and how you will test whether they have learned what you intended them to learn.

One of the best ways to share your expectations about the quality of student work is by providing students with scoring rubrics that specifically outline performance expectations. Give scoring rubrics to students at the start of a task so that they will know the criteria by which they will be evaluated. Students will perform to much higher levels if we can clearly share the criteria for success and teach our students to assess their own work. Rubrics are appropriate for students at all grade levels and should be written in "student-friendly" terms appropriate to their age level. If you have not used rubrics before or need tips about developing them, a number of helpful Web sites—such as www.rubrics4teachers.com, www.teach-nology.com/web_tools/rubrics, or www.rubrics.com—offer additional information and helpful tools for quickly and easily creating your own rubrics. Additional Web sites for rubrics are listed in Appendix B.

Next, we need to help students understand prompts. Teach students to underline or highlight key words such as *list, compare,* or *justify* as they read a constructed-response question. For example, students might need to provide "examples and illustrations" within the body of the response. If so, be sure that they highlight this fact so that they remember to do this. If formulas are needed to solve a problem, teach them to jot these down before they begin so that they can concentrate the rest of their thinking on organizing a response that meets the criteria of the prompt or question. Students must fully understand what they need to do to adequately answer the question before they can construct their response. Again, help students think through what a question is really asking by modeling this process orally with students. When they can do this on their own, they will be in a much better position of showing what they know and can do.

Once students have mastered being able to read a question and write a written response, it is time to teach them self-analysis and revision skills. Introduce scoring rubrics to your students at the beginning of the school year, demonstrating how to use them. A simple and fun way of helping students understand how to design a rubric is to ask them to work in groups to create a rubric for cleaning their own bedroom, scored from 0 to 5. Students of all ages can relate to this task and have a pretty thorough understanding of what the ranges would be from level 0 (which equals "No cleaning of the room at all") to 5 ("Mom's standard for cleaning when company is coming to visit"). For younger students with the intellectual understanding but not the motor skills to complete a written task, have students as a class brainstorm the criteria for the various scores as you record their ideas on the board. When they have completed their rubrics, ask students to rate their bedrooms' condition when they left for school that morning. This is sure to generate some hearty laughs and interesting comments! Students not only will have fun developing rubrics but also will quickly understand how rubrics can be used to evaluate their performance on a task. Once students become familiar with rubrics and how to use them, they can develop their own or help you develop a rubric for a class project or activity they will undertake.

Making the Invisible Visible

Once students understand the concept of how a rubric can help us analyze our performance, demonstrate for students how to score a written paragraph using the same talk-through methods you used earlier for reading a text passage. Model for students how to use a rubric to evaluate one's own work and how to see areas where they can go back and revise the work to strengthen it. Again, it is important that your students hear your thought processes as you self-analyze. This is what will make visible the invisible and will affect your students' performance.

Be sure to write paragraphs with various levels of complexity so your students can learn to analyze what is present and what is missing. Demonstrate how you might revise a passage to conform to a higher level by paying attention to what is missing in the passage. When possible, try to keep some of the students' work so that you can show examples of various levels—with names removed, of course. Again, forming students' skills in all of these areas takes time and practice. Allow many opportunities throughout the year for students to apply these skills over and over again with their work.

Determining a Rubric's Levels

The most frequently asked question about rubrics is, How many levels of discrimination should be built into a rubric? The simple answer is that there is no magical number; it entirely depends on the task and the level of performance expected. Perhaps the more specific question is, How many levels of discrimination do you need to differentiate an outstanding response from an average response from a poor response?

Consider the level of complexity best suited for a task. For some tasks, as many as six levels of performance might be more desirable, while for others, only three levels might suffice. Writing tasks, for example, often use a 5- or a 6-point rubric to allow for enough discrimination when scoring written papers. A rubric for solving a math problem might do well with only three levels of discrimination. In any case, open-ended questions scored with rubrics allow students to draw on their own knowledge, related background experience, and creativity to solve the problem in much higher-level ways than more restrictive forms of assessment.

If we examine the rubrics used by state scorers, we will see that state assessments typically use a score range of 3 to 6 points per constructed-response assessment question. With a 3-point rubric, for example, 3 points would be awarded for an "advanced" response, 2 points for an "average" response, and 1 point for a "minimal" response. When a student either does not respond at all or provides an answer that is not appropriate to the question, that student would receive 0 points.

Scoring rubrics can be based on the number of responses or on the quality of the response or a combination of both factors. Large complicated projects may be scored on several criteria, while more simple tasks may only need one criterion. Evaluating a story, for example, might need five or six criteria, while a task that simply asks a student to list three similarities between a whale and a dolphin might require a very simple rubric.

Evaluation Criteria: Include the "Wow" Level

Some people prefer to identify the criteria for the basic level (i.e., 0 points) and then move to the advanced level. Others opt to define the ideal response—the "wow" level—and then work backward from there. Either approach works as long as you concretely define the performance that corresponds to each level.

To build your evaluation criteria, first brainstorm examples of the responses that you believe students might make to the question. What might be typical responses? What points would constitute a basic response? How about an advanced response? What level of complexity shows deep thinking?

Scoring Guides

As students learn to apply the criteria in the rubric to scoring, they also learn how to improve their own work in very concrete ways. State tests often use two different types of scoring guides: one is based on the quality of a response, and the other is based on the quantity of responses. Examples of both types are presented here to help you develop your own rubrics.

Scoring Guide Based on Response Quality

Question: Explain how Captain Jim changed during the voyage at sea. Use examples and details from the story to support your answer.

4 points: The response is accurate, logical, and reasonably complete. The response provides several specific details, passages, and examples from the story to illustrate identified changes in the character. The response is well organized and presents a logical argument for the points cited.

3 points: The response is accurate but less complete, and it may be somewhat general or simplistic. Some reasoning may be provided, and the response may cite at least one example or detail to support any identified changes in the character. The response may be marginally organized or less convincing in argument. It lacks the overall depth and completeness present in a 4-point response.

2 points: The response is general and/or simplistic. It may be factually accurate but may fail to cite connections between character changes and details or examples from the story. The response may not flow logically or be well organized. It may cite events from the story rather than details about the changes of the character.

1 point: The response contains limited connections to the details of the story or gross inaccuracies. It does not identify any changes or significant details about the character of the captain. The response may recount memories associated with the topic but fails to address the prompt accurately. It is not well developed and does not have a logical flow.

0 points: The response does not address the prompt or refer to any details of the story or its characters. It is poorly constructed, illogical, or difficult to follow. The response may be off topic.

Scoring Guide Based on Response Quantity

Question: Explain how growing populations in a geographic area put pressure on the ecosystem of the area. Discuss at least four consequences, and use specific examples to support your arguments.

Topics discussed in the article that students might cite:

• Need for sources of additional clean, fresh water

• Need for additional food production but loss of farm land due to urbanization

• Toxic impacts on environment due to pollution from businesses and vehicles

• Impact of construction of roads, homes, and businesses on the environment

• Impact on natural habitats of wildlife due to encroachment on habitats

4 points: The response is accurate and logical, and it provides at least four reasons. It is well organized and includes specific examples to justify the points made.

3 points: The response is accurate and provides at least four responses, but the support may be less complete and developed. The response is not as well developed, and examples are limited or less convincing to support the argument. The response lacks the overall depth and completeness of a 4-point response.

2 points: The response is accurate but contains only two or three reasons, and it does not include any examples to demonstrate key points in the argument. It does not flow logically or is not well organized.

1 point: The response may give only one or two acceptable reasons and have few or no examples in support. It is not well developed and does not have a logical flow.

0 points: The response provides no acceptable reasons. It is poorly constructed, illogical, and/or difficult to follow. It may also be off topic.

Scoring Based on Quantity and Quality

Questions can also be developed that require a specific number of answers and also measure the quality of the response. An example of a question that would require both a quality and a quantity assessment would be the following:

Question: The Vietnam War was a costly war for the United States. Using the text from Chapter 19 in our textbook, explain whether you agree or disagree with this statement. Provide at least four specific reasons for your opinion and specific examples from the text to justify your position.

For a question like this that requires both quantity and quality in its response, you need to develop a blended scoring rubric. Begin by brainstorming acceptable answers as in the quantity rubric. After you've established the criteria for acceptable answers, develop criteria for the quality of the response as in the example of a quality scoring rubric. The following example of a 4-point scoring level demonstrates how the two types of scoring rubrics can be combined:

4 points: The response is accurate and logical, and it includes at least four reasons. It is well organized and provides several specific examples to justify the points made. The response is well organized and complete, and it presents a logical argument.

Rubrics as Performance-Raising Tools

Students should be provided with the scoring rubric at the start of the project or activity and taught to evaluate their own work against the rubric criteria. While using rubrics to help take the "guesswork" out of how students should prepare and justify their answers is not a new concept, regular use of rubrics in content classrooms is not as prevalent as it could be. Rubrics help students understand the various levels of performance associated with a task. They can provide high-quality feedback, involve students in self-assessment, and guide the depth of learning that students are expected to display. Students can also learn to use the rubric to critique the work of peers so that students can look at revision as a process of self-improvement where the "rules" are clearly established from the beginning of the task.

Learning to use a rubric as a yardstick of performance takes some of the guesswork out of performance requirements and helps students identify their weak areas more objectively. Teachers who help their students learn to self-evaluate and make improvement revisions on their own work report higher levels of student understanding and overall performance in content areas.

Terms and Vocabulary Reinforcement

Embedded in almost all state assessments are questions that ask students to define or provide synonyms for key vocabulary terms and important words in the content discipline. Because this testing strand cuts across all content areas, I have included a few strategies that apply to all content areas. Teachers can use these strategies to help students improve their mastery of key words and terms and their performance on assessments asking students to define or identify the meaning of specialized terms.

One of the most common types of questions on state exams is the multiple-choice question that asks students to consider a specific term and choose the best meaning for it. Help your students do well on these types of questions by teaching them how to use the context to determine word meanings. For example, you might say, "Look at the word _____ on page X of your text. What do you think this word might mean as it is used here?" When students respond, ask probing questions to find out what clues they used from the passage to determine the meaning: "How do you know? What details or information suggests to you that this might be the meaning of this word here?" Again, require students to respond with specific information and do not accept nonspecific answers.

Point out words in context, and ask students to think about what a word might mean. As they offer meanings, probe them to describe their thinking: "How did you figure that out?" or "What words or ideas in the sentence helped you unravel or identify that?" Deliberately thinking about how to decipher word meaning helps students apply these skills on a regular basis.

Another approach to helping students analyze vocabulary in context is by providing a structured format to do so, such as the following:

1. Look at the words before and after the word. Do they give you any clues?

2. Connect what you already know about this topic to what is said in this paragraph.

3. Predict the meaning that you think makes sense and reread the passage. Does the word you predict make sense in the context of the paragraph?

4. If not, rethink your idea and try a different meaning. Does it make sense?

5. If you still cannot understand the meaning of the word, either look it up or ask a resource who can help you.

6. When you understand the meaning of the word, go back and

reread the passage and make sure that you now understand the meaning of the paragraph.

For more strategies that help students determine a new word's meaning, see Marzano and Pickering's *Building Active Vocabulary* (2005).

"Mystery Word"

A fun way to help students learn to use context clues for vocabulary is the following strategy. Provide student partners with a new word in a context paragraph. Have the partners discuss what they think the word means and to write their own definition. After they have guessed what the word might mean, students look up the word in the dictionary, verifying that they have correctly understood its meaning. After making any corrections to their definition or synonyms, each pair has the teacher check their written notes for accuracy. Then each pair writes a very short story or dialogue of no more than eight sentences to illustrate the meaning of the word but *without* using the word directly in the story.

Now collect the stories and check them for accuracy and to ensure that each dialogue provides sufficient clues to unlock the mystery word. Return the paragraphs to the class, and ask the students to write the mystery word as the title. Then have them take turns writing their short story line by line on an overhead transparency. The story is shown one line at a time, with pauses after each line to allow for audience guesses as to the meaning of the mystery word. As students think they know its definition, they raise their hands to take a guess. When students correctly state the meaning, ask them to explain what clues or details they used to identify the mystery word. Again, it is not so much the right answer as being able to model thinking for other students that is important.

Vocabulary "Trivia"

Another fun way to help students learn important terms and vocabulary specific to your discipline is by creating a trivia card game out of the key terms and vocabulary items from your discipline. Make a list of the various terms, concepts, or key vocabulary words that your students are expected to understand or identify. For instance, examples in language arts might include knowing the characteristics of various genres; identifying settings, problems, or themes; describing the tone or mood of a piece; determining a main idea and the key details supporting that main idea; and defining various literary terms such as *personification, foreshadowing,* or other literary devices as appropriate to the age of your students. Each content area will have many ideas or words and phrases that students should know.

Once you have compiled the list, write each term or concept on an index card along with its definition. Create enough decks of cards so that each set of five to six students has a duplicate deck. Provide one deck of cards to each small group. Students take turns drawing a card and asking the person to the left to provide the correct definition or explanation. If the student gets the right answer, he or she gets to keep the card. If the student does not know the answer, the card is placed on the bottom of the deck, and the responder then draws a question to ask the next person in the circle. At the end of the allotted time frame or when all cards have been drawn, the cards are counted. The person with the most cards is declared the "winner" of the game. Students love the game and quickly learn the required definitions or vocabulary meanings that you want them to master.

Writing to Develop Vocabulary

One of the best instructional strategies that we can use to build our students' skills in developing responses and to improve their ability to express themselves and communicate their ideas is to incorporate lots of writing into every content course we teach. Just as students who read more become better readers, students who write more become better writers and communicators. Find ways to have students use reflective writing and thinking about the concepts they are learning, the questions they have, and the things they want to know. The more we can have students write about processes, procedures, the things they know, and the things that still confuse them, the better strategic thinkers they will become.

Test-Taking Tips That Help Students

Although much of test success depends on the quality of the instruction provided throughout the school year, a few strategies are helpful for students to know prior to taking an actual test. First, students pick up on our attitude toward the tests, even when we try not to overtly communicate our feelings. Thus, try to maintain an open, matter-of-fact attitude toward the evaluations you administer. Testing can be tedious, but it is a part of how the educational system works. Although we should encourage students to perform to the best of their abilities, students do better in an atmosphere of confidence and encouragement rather than one of tension and pressure.

Second, consider posting the suggestions listed here on the wall. Ask your students to review these hints every time you give them either a multiple-choice or a constructed-response exam. When regular instruction includes some of the same skills and activities that will appear on state assessments, students are comfortable and confident when they must take those tests.

Hints for Taking Multiple-Choice Tests

1. Do not linger too long on any question. Try to eliminate obviously wrong answers, mark your best guess, and move on. If time permits, return to questionable items later and review them.

2. Answer questions in order without skipping any questions. If you are unsure about your answer, either make a mark in the margin by that question, or, if you are not permitted to mark in the testing booklet, jot down the number of the question on scratch paper. Return to these questions if time permits, but change your answer only if you are absolutely sure that the response you have marked is incorrect. Often your first response is the correct one.

3. Reread all questions with negative wording such as *not* or *least*. Watch out for sentences that have double or triple negatives within the sentence. Look for words such as *all, most, none, some, always, usually, seldom,* or *never*. Additional words to note are *best/worst* or *smallest/largest*. When these words appear, the *entire* statement must be true for the response to be correct. Watch out for names, dates, places, or details that might appear in the statement that could make it inaccurate. Sometimes one detail will be changed in an otherwise-correct statement. Watch out for statements that have multiple ideas or concepts, since all parts of these must be true to be the correct answer.

4. Check for grammatical inconsistencies between the answer chosen and the question stem. A choice that does not match the stem is probably not the correct response.

5. When reviewing your responses, change an answer only if you have a valid reason for doing so. Remember, your first guess is often the correct one.

Hints for Taking Essay Tests

1. Read through the prompt, and immediately jot down all ideas, formulas, or pertinent facts that come to mind.

2. Estimate the amount of time that you will have to organize, develop, and refine your response, and keep track of your time so that you don't run out of time.

3. If you have more than one essay question, do the easier ones first if possible. If point values are indicated for the individual questions, respond to the questions that have the most points first.

4. Circle or underline the indicator words such as *define, list, compare, explain, identify, illustrate,* or *support* so that you know what it is that you are being asked to do in the essay.

5. Do not leave a question blank. Do your best to answer as much as you can even if you are not sure that it is correct. You might get a point or two even if you cannot correctly complete the entire response or solve the whole problem correctly.

6. If the prompt asks for "details," "information," or "support from the text," be sure you have included references directly from the text in your response.

7. If the prompt asks for a specific number of points, be sure that you have provided the correct number of points in your response.

8. Before you write, make a simple outline to organize your notes into a logical and sensible sequence. Quickly introduce your topic, and then spend your time getting the information presented and supported with details or examples if possible. Remember that to receive the maximum points, it is not how much you say but rather how well you present and support your viewpoint and give your information that matters.

9. If you are writing more than one essay, leave space so you can go back and add things that occur to you later. If you run out of time

while writing, outline the rest of your key points. It is better to get them down in some format than to leave them out altogether.

10. Write legibly in complete sentences and paragraphs. If you have time, reread your essay and correct any grammatical, spelling, or punctuation errors. Always use all of the time allocated to review and improve your essay. The more time you spend on your essay, the better your score is likely to be.

Constructed Response Improves Instruction and Student Learning

Once you have selected the learning standard to be measured, created the activity, presented and discussed the rubric, helped students understand the appropriate terms and vocabulary, and observed student performance, you should be able to identify the areas where students either individually or as a group may need more work. Constructed-response activities provide valuable insight into the skills and understandings that students can actually apply to problems or transfer to real-life situations. Many jobs—such as doctor, lab worker, realtor, carpenter, and even teacher—require individuals to demonstrate mastery of specific skills before they are allowed to have a license in their chosen field of employment. It seems reasonable that students, similarly, should be asked to go beyond merely selecting the multiple-choice bubble to demonstrate their understandings and should instead be asked to actually apply knowledge and understanding in a more authentic, hands-on task.

In the next chapters, we will look at examples of open-ended activities that can inspire you to create tasks that require students to use the skills of analysis, synthesis, evaluation, and interpretation as they learn and grow. The following chapters will help you understand various instructional strategies that invite students to think deeply and process information at the levels necessary for success both in the classroom and on state assessments. Chapters 3–6 are dedicated to each specific content area. If you only teach one content area, you may wish to read only that specific content chapter and then pick your reading back up in Chapter 7.

3 | Language Arts

Deepening Language Arts Instruction and Student Performance

Most state reading assessments are built around excerpts from works in the humanities (including prose fiction) as well as from nonfiction text taken directly from the social and natural sciences. Passages are designed to measure a student's ability to make a logical inference, analyze information, or synthesize information into a logical, cogent response. Some questions require using information found at the literal level, while many other questions require a deeper understanding and handling of more implicitly stated ideas and connections. In other words, students have to read text, analyze or synthesize what they have read, and then produce a response based on this thinking. Questions are designed so that students must apply several different skills to complete the acts of comprehending, interpreting, and evaluating various aspects of text. On most state tests, reading is measured as an active, reflective, and problem-solving process.

This chapter will discuss how language arts teachers can help students improve their performance on state reading assessments. Reading standards across the country are organized around the three types of text: literary, nonfiction, and technical. This means that language arts teachers need to expose students to all three types of text on a regular basis.

To learn more about what your students will be required to do at assessment time, closely examine the available information on assessment. Begin with a thorough analysis of your state standards as well as any sample test items that your state has released. (Appendix A lists Web sites to help you locate this information.) As you review available samples, be sure to take extensive notes about the genres and types of text your students will likely see on the exam. Will they encounter only fiction? Are some of the passages drawn from textbook-like passages in social studies or science? What genres are likely to be presented to students? Having a clear picture of the expectations will help you craft lessons that better prepare students for taking the tests. For example, if students are responsible for analyzing or responding to poetry on state assessments, be sure that working with poetry is frequently an instructional target throughout the school year. If tests will require that students describe a picture or write a story about what they see in a picture, then they should be asked to do these activities during the year. In most states, reading assessments at the elementary level will likely reflect a blend of literary, nonfiction, and technical text passages, so we must be careful to balance our instruction so that students have experience with each type of text. Assessments for middle and high school students will likely have a much heavier emphasis on nonfiction, content-based, and technical texts.

At an absolute minimum, students at all levels are expected to get the "big picture" or gist of the text while reading. They are expected to remember what they have read and to be able to make personal connections to the text even when they are choosing the best answer from a list of multiple-choice possibilities. Multiple-choice questions might ask students to select the "best title" for a passage, assess an author's general attitude toward a subject, or even predict what a character is likely to do next in a story. At higher performance levels, students will be asked to interpret meaning or analyze various aspects of the text. They might also be asked to evaluate the motives, actions, or changes in a specific character or even evaluate specific aspects of the author's craft or writing style. Examples of a constructed-response task that students might experience are the following:

Elementary: "Discuss how Billy changes from the beginning of the story to the end. Use examples from the text to support your response."

Secondary: "Myra's attitude changes several times over the course of the events in the story. Discuss the changes that occur and what prompted these changes. Use examples and illustrations from the text to support your response."

This type of question requires that students be able to critically read and analyze the text and then organize a meaningful response. It also requires that students choose ideas and statements with direct links to the text to support their essay. As we know, this is a complex task and a tall order for many students.

Reading assessment questions can be literal, as in the "right there" types of answers found specifically in the text, or they can be more global in nature, asking students to make some degree of inference from what is discussed in the text. Both types require students to use what reading experts often call "think and search" reading strategies. Because newer reading tests tend to use global questioning more frequently than literal questions, we must ensure that students develop the ability to grasp the entirety of what they are reading. It is critical that students learn to process text holistically and respond to what they read. This chapter describes many strategies to build these skills on a daily basis. By regularly performing tasks that mirror what is required on state assessments, our students will become better prepared to apply their knowledge and skills at assessment time.

Using State Test Design to Guide Instruction

No matter the state, reading tests typically focus on four text elements:

- Main idea or supporting details
- Some facet of the author's craft or writing style
- Relationships (sequential, comparative, or cause and effect)
- Generalizations or conclusions

In addition, almost all reading tests ask students to identify the meaning of vocabulary words by using surrounding context to choose the appropriate definition. If students respond to these four text elements on a regular basis during daily instruction, the items on state tests will be familiar and comfortable for them.

In many states, reading tests consist of two parts: a multiple-choice section and a section where students develop their own, longer responses. On the multiple-choice portion, students must select the correct answer from four or five provided statements. The constructed-response part may be short-answer questions, where students are asked to write a few sentences based on a specific text passage, or essay questions, where students are asked to respond by developing an original, well-organized essay based on the selected text. Together, the multiple-choice and constructed-response items produce the score the student will receive on the reading subtest.

If your state has not yet included any constructed-response items on the state reading assessment, it is highly likely that it will at the next revision. The heavier the test is on constructed-response items, the more difficult it is for students. For this reason, it is essential that all teachers understand how to help students maximize their performance on assessments that contain multiple-choice as well as constructed-response questions.

Understanding what students will need to do is the first step toward improving student performance. Let's drill down and take a look at the kinds of multiple-choice and constructed-response items typically found on state reading assessments.

Responding to Global Questions

A quick analysis of multiple-choice items shows us that many of the questions require a comprehensive or "global" level of understanding of the text the student has read. Global questions require that the student be able to understand the text, summarize the information to obtain the general gist the author is trying to convey, and then synthesize this information into some type of response.

Global questions are often put into multiple-choice formats since they are fairly simplistic and are derived directly from the text content. Some typical global questions on a reading subtest are as follows:

• "Select the best title for the passage."

- "According to the passage, why was Mary unhappy?"
- "Paragraph 2 is mainly about. . . ."
- "Peter didn't want to go home because. . . ."
- "Which statement is an example of an author's opinion?"

In each case, students must think about the overall meaning of the text to choose the right answer from four to six possibilities.

When presented with several specific choices, many students are able to filter the responses and identify the correct answer. Had these students simply been asked to construct an answer without the benefit of any additional clues, they may not have been able to accurately complete the task. They may have some understanding of the gist of the paragraph, but their comprehension does not extend to the application, analysis, synthesis, or evaluation level. This happens because although students are used to identifying a correct answer, they have not been taught to apply their thinking at the deepest levels.

Global questions can also form the basis for short-answer assessment questions where the student is expected to respond with a few brief sentences. Some examples of short-answer global questions might be the following:

Elementary: "Identify from the passage three reasons why people headed west toward California in 1849."

Elementary: "According to the story, name three things that Tammy and Laurie have in common."

Secondary: "According to the article, what are three factors that may be contributing to global warming?"

Secondary: "If April were to find money in the future, predict what she might do with the money. Use examples from the story to support your viewpoint."

To prepare our students to easily respond to these types of questions, we can use specific instructional strategies every day. Instead of simply asking students to answer questions about text passages from memory, we should teach students to go back and skim articles to find explicit information in the passage. Instead of simply accepting a response, ask students to provide the page number and the paragraph where the information can be found as they respond. In this way, students will get used to scanning text to find the important information supporting their ideas. This will be useful on state tests.

We can also deepen student understanding of text by asking students to summarize the gist of the articles they read. One good way to help students understand how to summarize information is to demonstrate the thinking a good reader uses during this process by displaying and reading to the class a short article on the overhead. After you've read the article, turn off the overhead and ask students to tell you what the article was about so that you can write a paragraph summarizing the information. Start by listing key details that the students remember from the article. If necessary, turn on the overhead only to verify a missing detail or fact that is needed. Once the students have listed most of the key facts, ask them to help you organize the information into a meaningful paragraph or two about the topic of the article. Provide additional modeling and practice until students can easily write the gist of text by themselves. This strategy will help students learn how to summarize text and also how to paraphrase research rather than copying it verbatim from a source.

Give students frequent opportunities to locate information, cite page and paragraph, and summarize the gist of articles they read whenever possible. Ask them to begin writing several sentences or a paragraph or two to summarize what they read each time they read text. Have students share their summaries and discuss the traits that make a good summary. By asking students to think about a passage and boil it down to a few key ideas, you are helping them learn to process text at the global level.

Make the Connections Personal

The second type of question on state assessments asks students to make a personal connection to text. Students are often asked to use the information in the text to form an opinion or make a connection based on their own background knowledge. Although personal response questions can be found on multiple-choice sections of state reading tests, they are more commonly found in short-answer or more complex constructed-response sections where the student will write a few brief sentences or a longer essay. Here are some typical examples of short-answer constructed-response questions on state reading assessments:

Elementary: "How can the reader tell that Jim cares about his family?"

Elementary: "How does the reader know that Sam doesn't like Pete?"

Secondary: "Explain the mixed feelings Kelly has about moving."

Secondary: "What do you think Ben learned by the end of the story?"

To respond, students are expected to use personal knowledge to put themselves in the character's shoes to interpret the character's actions, feelings, and motivations. In all probability, the information would be inferential, and students would have to use their own personal understandings and connections to make the interpretations and provide an acceptable response. Depending on the length of the text, these types of questions generally have a limited range of acceptable responses.

In addition to identifying the character's feelings or motivation, the prompt may also ask students to provide examples and information from the text to support their ideas and conclusions. Here are some additional examples of personal connection questions that might require more comprehensive responses:

Elementary: "Have you ever been in a situation where you felt alone and afraid?"

Elementary: "Would you enjoy staying in the Hooka Village? Cite four reasons from the text to justify your answer."

Elementary: "If you lived in Ireland during the potato famine of the 1840s, would you have immigrated to another country? Use information from the passage to explain why or why not."

Elementary: "After reading this article, would you have liked to live during colonial times? What information makes you think this? Cite information from the text to support your response."

Secondary: "What kind of person is Patagonia in this poem?"

Secondary: "Explain how life for Melissa and Amy is alike or different. Use examples from the story to support your answer."

In each case, students must use the text information along with their own personal background knowledge and experience to develop a response. In many cases, they also need to support their answer by making links back to the story or by citing information directly from the text. You can help students develop familiarity with responding to these types of questions by asking them to do these tasks orally and by frequently modeling your own connections to text. Ask students to think about ways that they are like the characters in the text or how their lives are affected by information that they read.

Students like to talk about themselves, so getting them to relate their own experiences to text is a helpful way to prepare them to answer questions that require them to make personal connections to the text. Some examples of such constructed-response items include the following:

Elementary: "If a new friend from Africa asked you about your three favorite hobbies and why you liked those things, what would you say?"

Secondary: "After reading the article about the environment, list several things that you can do as an individual to affect the environment in your own town."

Allowing students time to talk about the things that happen to characters in a story and then relate these experiences to their own lives is a powerful tool to use in the language arts classroom. No matter what students' cultural background or experiences may be, we can help students relate to the characters' emotions and problems by giving them some time to think about and discuss the text in meaningful ways with their peers. Struggling readers often move through a text without stopping to really think about the characters' actions and experiences and whether those experiences make sense to them. Helping students think about and relate to the characters and the events happening in the text can substantially increase student comprehension.

According to Keene and Zimmerman (1997), comprehension improves when students can relate text to themselves and to other texts they are reading, as well as to the larger world around them. While reading stories, articles, and poems, ask students for their opinions with questions like these:

- "Did Character X's actions make sense to you in that scene?"
- "Would you enjoy doing. . . ? Why or why not?"
- "Would you have acted like Character X in this situation? Why or why not?"
- "Has anything like that ever happened to you or to someone you know?"
- "How did you feel as you were reading that?"
- "In what ways are you like (or different from) Character X?"
- "What three questions would you ask Character X if she were in our class today?"
- "Who can tell me a couple of ways that Character X can solve the problem he faces in the story?"
- "How would Character X handle things if he lived in your own neighborhood? Give me some examples from the story to support your viewpoint."
- "Describe the relationship of Character X to Character Y. Give some examples from the text to support your opinions."

Ask students to make brief notations on sticky notes and place them in their books as they are reading whenever they can make a personal connection to the text. Provide time for students to share these connections with you and with small groups of other students from time to time. Encourage students to compare and contrast their own lives with the lives and events in the stories they are reading and to ask questions of one another about things they did not understand in the text. Being able to discuss text with peers can be beneficial to struggling readers as well as to students for whom English is a second language. Once students are comfortable orally making personal connections, begin giving them opportunities to use graphic organizers such as Venn diagrams or compare/contrast charts to list their observations in a more organized and deliberate way. Gradually, with modeling and thinking aloud, move your students to writing a paragraph or two about the characters with specific examples pulled from the text to show their connections and ideas. By constantly practicing making personal connections to text, students will easily develop the skills needed to excel on this type of constructed-response question. Students who are often asked to formulate their own connections to people, places, and events in the text they are reading are well prepared to do the same at assessment time.

Interpretive Questions

The third type of question commonly found on state assessments requires students to examine the information and combine it with what they already know about a topic to synthesize or interpret a response. Interpretive responses are not explicitly stated in the text but require students to make interpretations about the information to answer the question. In many cases, these types of questions require a more in-depth answer. As a result, they are frequently used for short-answer or more lengthy responses rather than in multiple-choice sections. Here are examples of an interpretive question:

Elementary: "What is wrong with Adisu and Cohen's thinking in the story? List three details or examples from the story to support your conclusions."

Elementary: "Will Jack and his teacher ever get to like each other? Use examples and details from the story to support your answer."

Secondary: "Describe what you think Laura will do next. Provide reasons to justify your answer."

Secondary: "How does the reader know that Jim often goes diving? Cite specific information from the passage that helps the reader understand this."

Questions of this type require the highest level of thinking and processing because students must draw conclusions from both explicit and implicit information. In most cases, these responses can require a much longer, more open-ended response since students will also be asked to draw information from the passage to support or justify their ideas. In many cases, the response will be scored on whether the student has presented a plausible explanation that is supported with concrete evidence from the text.

Constructed Response and
Higher-Order Thinking Demands

Many students have a basic level of understanding that allows them to identify a correct answer from a given set of multiple-choice responses. Being asked to synthesize information, arrive at an analysis, and formulate an organized response that meets specific criteria is where performance falls apart for many students. While each of the three types of questions discussed so far could be formatted as a multiple-choice, a fill-in-the-blank, or a more demanding constructed-response item, some types of questions lend themselves better to essay response formats than to multiple-choice formats or fill-in-the-blank formats. Essay questions require a much higher level of critical thinking and a deeper level of understanding on the part of the respondent. This is the level of thinking where students encounter the most difficulty. As a result, we must make a special effort to build student familiarity and capability in this area.

Commonly found questions on reading assessments that fit these characteristics ask students to analyze and respond to an author's purpose, perspective, ideas, character development, or other aspects of the writer's craft. Questions in this area that might appear as essay-type constructed-response items on a state assessment may be similar to the following:

Elementary: "Is Grandpa really a grouchy old man, or is he really a softie? Give details and examples from the text to support your point of view."

Elementary: "Choose several actions that Barry did in the story, and discuss what it tells about his character. Provide information from the text to support your opinion."

Secondary: "Discuss the author's purpose in writing this story. Support your ideas with details and examples from the text."

Secondary: "In this passage from *Watership Down,* the author makes us feel like the animals are human. Does this humanization make the story seem unrealistic, or does it make it more meaningful to the reader? Give examples from the text to support your opinion."

Secondary: "Discuss how the author shows that Harry has grown up during the story. Give details and examples from the story to support your point of view."

Secondary: "The character in this story changed significantly over the course of the story. Discuss these changes, citing evidence from the story that shows key turning points in the character's beliefs and attitudes."

As is evident from the complexity of these questions, students will need many skills and the ability to make a complex analysis of the text to respond correctly. Not only must students understand the gist of the text, but they must be able to delve deeper and gain insights far beyond where superficial readings might lead them. When we plan our lessons, we strive for this level of performance.

Do More with Less

The three levels at which students should be trained to read are as follows:

1. What the text says—students write a summary to show understanding.

2. How the text is organized—students pull out examples and illustrations or arguments or contrast viewpoints to clarify information.

3. What it means—students seek the interpretation of a text and make connections.

Often students read superficially and think that they have understood a text. We can call this the "I read it and now I'm done" attitude. Get students into the habit of "revisiting" text by rereading and visiting text with multiple eyes. One reading might look at personal connections; the next might be from an interpretive or critical perspective on the point the author was trying to make. Do more with less to deepen student understanding.

Know what the expectations are for your grade level. Are students expected to identify genres? Must they be able to identify mood, tone, or theme? Do they need to understand and be able to identify examples of personification? Will they need to identify the main idea of a text and be able to provide supporting details? Do they need to analyze how an author writes or develops the characters in the text? Once you understand the skills that students will be expected to demonstrate, then students should practice these skills regularly so that there abilities are well honed by the time they are expected to apply these same skills on a state assessment.

Students must learn to reflect and analyze text deeply to answer the most complex type of constructed-response questions. When students are routinely asked to perform at levels above where they need to be for state assessments, teachers don't have to worry or wonder how students will score on those instruments. They will already know that their students can perform well on the tasks they will be required to do.

Determining the Author's Purpose

Another skill that students frequently need on constructed-response language arts items is determining the author's purpose. Help students understand that the author's purpose in writing text is simply the answer to this question: "What does the author most want me to learn from this text?" To help students learn to think about this idea, ask them to carefully think about the title of the book, article, or excerpt. Does the title provide any idea about what the author wants readers to learn from this text? Students should then read the text and complete the following details:

I think the author's purpose in writing (title) _____ is to

_____

_____

_____

Some of the details that prove this to me are _____

_____

_____

_____

Figure 3.1 lists some common author purposes and the forms of writing they can take.

FIGURE 3.1
Author Purpose

Author Purpose for Creating Text	Forms of Writing Commonly Used
To amuse someone	Stories; poems; jokes; riddles; puzzles; dramatic scripts; fictional books; comic books; song lyrics; picture books; personal anecdotes
To clarify thinking	Jotting; journals; diaries; note taking; explanations
To describe	Reports; labels; captions; biographies or character portraits; advertisements; textbooks; diaries; catalogs
To establish or maintain relationships with someone else	Letters; greeting cards; questionnaires; e-mails; instant messaging; thank-you notes
To gather information	Interviews; notes; surveys; questionnaires
To inform or advise	Posters; advertisements; newscasts; minutes of meetings; invitations; programs for events; nonfiction books or articles; manuals; textbooks; letters; legal documents; newspapers; magazines
To make comparisons	Charts; graphs; diagrams; descriptions
To persuade	Advertisements; commercials; infomercials; letters to the editor; notes for a debate; cartoons
To predict or hypothesize	Scientific hypothesis or experiment reports; ideas about events yet to happen; questions to guide research or an interview
To provide directions	Recipes; instructions; stage directions in a play script; rules; maps; manuals
To record feelings and observations	Personal letters; science experiment reports; poems; doodling; song lyrics; plays; diaries; journals

Helping Students Improve Thinking and Inferencing Skills

One of the most difficult tasks for students who struggle with reading or for whom English is a second language is making good inferences. *Inferences* are educated guesses based on our own background knowledge and the evidence we see. For example, we infer people are thirsty if they ask for a glass of water, tired if they yawn, happy if they are smiling, or cold if they are putting on a sweater or a coat. In fact, our students infer what kind of mood we are in the moment they walk through the classroom door each day.

Making an inference is a thought process by which we come to a conclusion based on the information we have received while reading or observing. We infer information about events that are happening and the motives and intentions of other people, as well as the meaning things have for us. We accept or reject information based on our interpretations of these observations.

Inferential comprehension is the ability to think beyond what is directly stated or to "read between the lines." It is the ability to understand what is directly said as well as to gather information about what is not said directly but is understood. People with good inferential comprehension skills can think more deeply about the meaning of text and what they are reading. They can develop insights and draw conclusions that others may miss. They can answer questions that come from insights beyond the literal. Some examples of questions that meet this description are

- "What kind of a person is Kelly?"
- "Have you ever felt like Mary?"
- "Do you think Peter is a sincere person? Why or why not?"

Each of these questions requires students to consider the things the character has said, how the action of the story has been presented by the author, and how other characters respond to the character in question.

Sometimes we settle for superficial comprehension when a more thorough understanding of less material would produce more quality thinking and learning. Asking open-ended questions like these can get students thinking more deeply to determine that they are really making sense of the text and can make connections with the events and people being depicted. For example, ask students, "Why do you think Character X said. . . ?" or "Why would Character Y think. . . ?" Many assessments' constructed-response questions will ask students to go beyond the literal and into the inferential realm, so the more you can train students to make these connections, the stronger their responses will be.

How Can We Help Struggling Readers Make Inferences?

In text, we must make inferences only from what the author tells us or from the actions attributed to each character. Since we don't have the advantage of observing body language, making inferences from only words is a much more difficult task. Good readers make inferences by comparing the words they see or hear with their own background knowledge, social customs, and communication patterns. We make sense of text by using this background knowledge to recognize implications and draw conclusions.

Although struggling readers frequently have difficulty grasping inferences in written passages, this does not mean that they lack skill in this area. These students are often highly skilled in watching and interpreting what goes on in their own personal environment since their very survival may depend on doing so. Because reading is sometimes slow and laborious for these students, problems with fluency may be preventing them from identifying the same clues that they would readily pick up visually. We often find that struggling readers have not learned to visualize things in their minds while reading. Without the ability to visualize what is happening, they often miss the subtle clues that would otherwise provide them with information about the events taking place. A good way to help these students is to read orally to them with short breaks every three to four paragraphs to summarize what is happening. Ask probing questions like these:

- "What is Character X feeling, and how do you know?"
- "Why do you think Character Y is doing this?"
- "How do you think he knew that?"

When students can identify these clues orally, they are ready to move to reading text and trying to do the same thing on their own. Provide these students with short descriptive passages to read that require making inferences. Ask them to illustrate with drawings what is happening as the story progresses. This will help them improve comprehension by thinking about and visualizing the text they are reading. The following passage is an example of a text that would be good to ask struggling readers to read and illustrate. As students read, tell them to try to visualize the events happening just as if they were watching a movie in their heads:

> Bobby's horse was running well today—in fact, better than ever before. He had passed many of the other horses on the field by the time he came down the home stretch. As the bell sounded, Bobby threw his popcorn high into the air, let out a happy whoop filled with all of the pent-up excitement he had been holding, and hugged his father with all of his might.

Look at the students' drawings to see if they have made the correct connections. Ask questions like "Where are Bobby and his father?" "What happened at the beginning of the story?" and "What happened at the end?" After each question, ask students to talk about the details that gave them clues on how to interpret each thing that happened. Tell students that reading is like solving a puzzle with their minds just as they do with their eyes while looking at a situation. Continue the process of stopping and asking struggling readers to practice sketching out what they are seeing in their minds whenever the text lends itself to making inferences and drawing conclusions.

Another good idea for helping students improve their visualization skills is to provide short, highly visual poetry such as haiku. Read the poem aloud, and ask students to draw a picture of the scene or object the author is describing. Again, the more students practice visualizing what is described in text, the better they will become at grasping the meaning of text.

Analyzing Characters

Another complex task that students are asked to do on constructed-response questions is to analyze characters from a critical perspective. Consider these sample questions:

Elementary: "Explain how Melissa and Amy are alike and different. Use examples from the story to support your answer."

Secondary: "Explain how the families of Romeo and Juliet are alike and different. Use examples from the story to support your answer."

Secondary: "Mr. Frump and Ms. Scott each have different viewpoints with regard to money. Compare and contrast these two viewpoints. Use examples from the text to support your response."

Let's first examine what skills a student might need to write an effective response at the elementary level. First, students must be able to read and summarize the story they have been asked to read. If they cannot summarize the text in a meaningful way, they will find it difficult to use the information to draw conclusions or make comparisons. In this case, summarization is a foundational skill for being able to compare and contrast characters or elements of a story.

Next, our students must be able to identify personal characteristics. What vocabulary is appropriate for describing people? How do we compare people? How will students organize their ideas? Do students know how to use graphic organizers to organize their thoughts? Will students need to make inferences, or is all of the information explicitly stated in the text? What skills do students still need to effectively draw conclusions or make inferences?

Once they have outlined the similarities and differences, students will have to write an organized essay and be able to include specific information from the text to support their viewpoint. Do students understand how to construct an accurate, logical, and well-organized paragraph to present their thoughts and ideas? Do students know how to select passages that demonstrate their point of view? Do they know how to appropriately cite information from the text to support their ideas and conclusions? When we break the task down into the component parts, we can quickly see where we will need to spend additional preparation time helping students develop the skills required to respond well on their state assessments. Using your knowledge about the students you teach, you can design activities to take your students from where they are to where they will need to be. Clearly, this progress will not happen without focused instruction and guided practice throughout the year.

Now, let's take that same basic question and move it up to a secondary level. At this level, students may need to be able to use more literary terms to compare and contrast main characters. They may need to understand literary terms like *round* versus *flat characters, antagonist* versus *protagonist,* or other such literary concepts. Again, your state standards should help you identify what terms, concepts, and understandings your students will need at assessment time. Students will also need a more sophisticated vocabulary to describe character traits than they do at the elementary level. To make comparison statements at the secondary level, students may need to understand character descriptors such as *gullible, unforgiving, negative,* or *trustworthy,* to name just a few. They will also need to understand how to analyze how the author presents or develops the characters as the narration unfolds. On some state assessments, such as those in California, one of the delineators between a "strong" response (which might earn 3 out of 4 possible points) and an "outstanding" response (which earns all 4 possible points) is the sophistication of the student's vocabulary. By helping students expand their descriptive vocabulary, you are likely also helping them raise their performance level.

Just as the elementary students did, secondary students will also need to know how to organize their thoughts, identify similarities and differences, and select appropriate references that support their point of view. They will be expected to present a logical argument that is accurate, organized, and convincing. As we plan our instruction, the answers to each of these questions will guide the depth of our teaching. With guided practice and thorough feedback that shapes their abilities, we can help our students learn to effectively respond to such questions as accurately and completely as possible.

Compare and Contrast Questions

State assessments often ask students to make comparisons such as these:

• "Describe a family tradition that takes place in your family. Discuss how it is similar to or different from the traditions in the Eskimo home."

• "Compare what school is like for you with what school is like for Meiko. Use details and examples from the story to support your response."

• "Analyze how Character X would adapt to life if he lived in your neighborhood. Use ideas or examples from the story to support your viewpoint."

• "Describe the relationship of Character X to Character Y. Use examples from the story to support your opinions."

The Role of Strong Vocabulary

Let's begin by thinking about how we can help students learn to compare and contrast two characters more effectively. In my experience, one of the biggest reasons that students have trouble comparing characters is that their "trait descriptor" vocabulary is limited. While students "describe" other people such as their parents, their teachers, and their peers all of the time, the vocabulary they use is not the same one that will "win friends and influence scoring judges" in a positive manner. For this reason, the first step in preparing students to compare and contrast people is to ensure that your students have the vocabulary and concept understanding to be able to identify personal traits both in themselves and for characters in text. Even advanced students can always use more work in this area since vocabulary can always be enlarged. Remember, vocabulary may be all that separates an "acceptable" and a "superior" score.

Let's look at some examples of how we might help students build background knowledge in this area. Ask students to brainstorm, either as a class or in small groups, all of the words they know that can describe people. Be sure that students can give examples or explanations to illustrate more difficult concepts that are named. This activity will help you diagnose which words your students already have in their background knowledge and which words you might want to introduce. Although the following list is by no means exhaustive, it includes some common examples of character descriptors your students should know:

active	cowardly	generous	irreverent
affectionate	creative	gentle	jealous
aloof	cruel	gossipy	jolly
ambitious	decent	graceful	kindhearted
angry	depressed	gracious	lazy
anxious	diabolical	grateful	lenient
appreciative	dishonest	greedy	likable
beautiful	disorganized	gregarious	lively
boisterous	dissatisfied	grouchy	lonely
bold	dreamer	grumpy	loud
boring	dull	hateful	loving
bossy	easygoing	healthy	loyal
brave	educated	heartless	lucky
bright	emotional	helpless	mean
careless	encouraging	honest	meek
casual	entertaining	horrible	merciless
cheerful	excitable	humble	messy
clever	exiting	humorous	mischievous
clumsy	fair	hyperactive	modest
complainer	flamboyant	impatient	moody
compliant	flashy	impolite	morbid
compulsive	foolish	impulsive	motivating
conceited	forgetful	inconsiderate	mulish
conniving	forgiving	inquisitive	mysterious
considerate	friendly	insistent	nasty
cooperative	frightened	inspiring	naughty
courageous	fun-loving	intelligent	negative
courteous	gabby	irrational	nervous

noble	realist	smart	thoughtful
noisy	rebellious	sociable	tidy
nonconforming	resentful	spirited	tolerant
nosy	responsible	spiteful	treacherous
obedient	revengeful	spoiled	troublemaker
obnoxious	reverent	squeamish	trustworthy
odd	ridiculous	stately	two-faced
optimistic	rude	stern	uncooperative
orderly	sad	stingy	unforgiving
patient	self-assured	strange	unfriendly
patronizing	sensible	strong	vain
peaceful	serious	studious	vengeful
persistent	shy	superstitious	vindictive
pessimistic	silly	supportive	warm
playful	sincere	sweet	weak
pleasant	sinister	swindler	well behaved
polite	skillful	sympathetic	whiner
prejudiced	sloppy	talkative	wild
quiet	sly	thankful	witty
			worried

The Shift to Writing

Since students can relate concepts to themselves more directly, begin by asking them to self-reflect and to create a list of adjectives that describe their own personality traits. A good way to do this is to use sentence completion statements that describe an action and then justify the label by showing how this is expressed. This helps students use the term and also shows that they understand the meaning of the trait. For example, "I am _____ because _____ _____ ."

A student might write, "I am <u>fair</u> because <u>I always listen to all sides of an argument before making up my mind about a problem</u>."

Allow students to discuss their personal characteristics and their justifications with one another in small groups so that they gain a thorough understanding of the terms being introduced. Teach students how to use a rubric to evaluate their own work as well as their peers'. Provide example or anchor papers that help students understand why one paper received a high score while another lost some points for missing information. When students begin to self-analyze, they can then begin to identify what is needed for their own improvement. A sample of a rubric that might be helpful as secondary students evaluate their own work is presented in Figure 3.2.

To move this activity to the next level, allow students to think about other people they know and to write sentence descriptions about these individuals in the same format. After working with the descriptors and discussing them with peers for a week or two, students should have a good understanding of how to apply character traits to characters from stories they are reading. As students read, ask them to think about the personal traits of the characters and to "find evidence" of actions or statements that show or "prove" that the character exhibits these traits in the text. Ask students to locate examples and mark these passages with sticky notes so that they can share their observations later during class discussions. Have students discuss their observations orally as a class. Guide the discussion with questions such as "What sort of person is Character X, and what proof do you have of this?" During discussion, students must now provide specific examples from the text that show how this character has acted in a manner that is characteristic of the trait they say the character displays. Encourage students to agree or disagree with one another, but again, require "proof" by requesting a specific page and paragraph as an example. Each time students provide the page and paragraph citations, flip to this section of the text and read the passages together. Ask students to determine if they agree or disagree that the character displays those traits based on the "evidence."

Class Discussion That Fosters Deep Thinking

Students who are really learning the information at deep levels can respond by asking questions, making contributions to a discussion, and paraphrasing for someone else what is being discussed. As the teacher, your role is simply to facilitate the class discussion and to keep

---

FIGURE 3.2
Character Traits Student Rubric

Targeted Student Rubric

Character Descriptors:

4 Points: I am able to list at least three character traits that describe each of the characters named in the question. I have cited at least three relevant actions or passages that provide evidence that supports my evaluation of each character.
3 Points: I am able to list one or two character traits that describe each of the characters. I have cited one or two relevant actions or passages that provide evidence to support my evaluation of each character.
2 Points: I am able to list a few character traits, but I have not made any connections to the text or provided support for my ideas.
1 Point: I am having difficulty identifying the character traits of the characters named in the question. I will need to ask for additional help to develop my skills in this area.

My Self-Assessment _____   Teacher Assessment _____

Paragraph Construction:

4 Points: My paragraph is clear, well organized, and logically presents my ideas and conclusions.
3 Points: My paragraph presents my ideas and conclusions but needs more clarity or organization to strongly persuade others of my ideas or my point of view.
2 Points: My paragraph needs more work to convince others that I have logically supported, strong ideas.
1 Point: I need additional support to develop a well-organized paragraph to support my thoughts and ideas.

My Self-Assessment _____   Teacher Assessment _____

---

the conversation moving along at a brisk and lively pace. Try to refrain from expressing your own opinion whenever possible because this can be a "discussion stopper." Students have come to expect teachers to be the "authority," so any comments we make or opinions we express may shut down any further discussion.

Remind students to try to look at the arguments and the evidence only to form their opinions and judgments. Encourage them to disagree with one another, but teach them to do so amiably and politely by using statements such as "I understand your position, but I disagree with you because. . . ." Teach students that we are all entitled to our own opinions as long as we can base them on logical assumptions. Accept all opinions that can be supported with "proof" from the text regardless of whether you agree with the interpretation. Simply say, "OK, you could look at it that way." The freedom to express their thoughts and feelings may be unfamiliar to some students, so allow time for them to get comfortable with the process. After students know that you will respect their thoughts and opinions and they feel safe presenting them, more and more students will choose to participate in discussions around text.

Once students are easily using an evidence-based approach and participating in lively whole-class discussions, deepen their learning and participation by moving to a small-group format of five to eight students per discussion group. Ask students to create "rules for operation" for each group to ensure that their group will function effectively. Remind students to be respectful of the speaker and to dispute only what is verifiable in the text. Never allow students to verbally attack one another or to make personal comments. At the beginning, provide a set of written, open-ended, "guiding questions" for the group to discuss that are similar to the questions you prepared for your own oral discussion. Circulate around the room, take notes on what you observe, and monitor group performance. If a group is struggling, sit with those students to facilitate the discussion for a while. After the students get comfortable with discussing text in a small-group format, some will begin moving past the written questions to have more authentic or "real" conversations about text. Students who can do this have no trouble responding to state assessments that require them to do the same type of analysis.

Using Graphic Organizers to Construct Meaning

Many state assessments ask students to organize their thinking by graphically representing textual information. Students might be asked to make a T comparison chart, create a web showing various relationships, show the sequence of events in the story, list facts and supporting details, or identify the key elements of the story. By asking students to regularly use these tools when they encounter text, they will also be comfortable using them to analyze and categorize text and information at assessment time. Many good assessments and strategies for reading can be found in my earlier books: *Threads of Reading: Strategies for Literacy Development* (2003) and *Literacy Strategies for Grades 4–12: Reinforcing the Threads of Reading* (2005). Educational supply stores will have many good books for each content area as well. Appendix B also provides many Web links to hands-on simulations and other fun resources to use in the language arts classroom.

Graphic organizers must be taught as tools. Students should understand why certain graphic organizers work for certain types of information so they can select the right tools for the job. While I have used teacher-led, evidence-based discussion groups from the 4th grade level up, elementary students in particular benefit from being able to record their thinking about various character traits visually on appropriate graphic organizers. Venn diagrams, compare/contrast T-charts, and other such graphic organizers can help students identify similarities and differences and clarify their thinking before they begin to write about these traits (see Figure 3.3). Once students have listed the information on graphic organizers, model by demonstrating and thinking aloud how to use this information to create a well-written response to explain a conclusion. Ask students to practice this skill on a frequent basis so they can easily perform this task.

Another way to help students think about characters in a more complex way is by asking them to create a character portrait pie chart—a large circle divided into six sections. Students write about the various aspects as listed in the following questions and then put a few words or pictures on the pie chart to create a portrait of the character they are analyzing.

Questions for the pie chart might include the following:

• Describe: What does the character look like? What are his or her likes/dislikes? What is unique or special about this character?

• Apply: What is the character's role in the novel? What information in the story proves this?

FIGURE 3.3	
Similarities and Differences	
Character Similarities and Differences for _____ **and** _____	**Proof from the Text That Tells Me This**
Similarities:	Proof:
Differences:	Proof:

• Compare: How is the character you have selected similar to or different from other characters in the story? What parts of the story show this?

• Analyze: What is the character's goal or motivation? What problems does the character face? How does he or she feel about things? What proof can you find in the story of this?

• Associate: Whom or what does this character make you think of? Who is like this character? How are they alike or different?

• Argue: Do you like or dislike the character? What about the character makes you feel this way? Cite examples or illustrations in the story to support your viewpoint.

Teaching Students to Analyze the Author's Craft

For many students, the most difficult type of constructed-response question is one that requires them to put themselves in the author's shoes or to analyze some aspect of the writer's craft. Questions in this area can ask students to judge the author's purpose in writing a piece; to examine elements of the work such as plot, climax, or resolution; or to identify the literary elements such as mood or tone in a text. Students might also be asked to evaluate the language the author uses or a specific aspect of the writer's craft such as the vocabulary style, the use of flashbacks, or the imagery presented in the text. They may be asked to analyze character development by reflecting on changes in personality, thinking, or actions in a story. To successfully respond to these types of questions, students will need many opportunities to analyze the author's craft.

Help students become more aware of language in the texts they are reading. As students read stories and books, ask them to find places in the text where they like the sound of the words or they are struck by the writing. Have them place sticky notes at these locations with a couple of connection words that can help them recall why they chose the word. Ask students to share these words and discuss why they like the word or were struck by the word while reading. Get kids talking about why authors choose the types of words they do. What do the words convey? What tone or mood do these words convey to the reader? Children's picture books are good sources to use to help students understand author craft because they can be examined in short segments of time. Help students classify the nature of language choices by categorizing words and looking for patterns of word choice in the texts they are reading. Find authors who have written a number of short picture books such as Mercer Mayer, Tommy De Paolo, Eric Carle, Ralph Fletcher, or even Dr. Seuss. Students can zero in on the author's craft by studying a specific element such as "creating imagery" or "using dialogue" in a picture book.

Choose several complementary books, and have students compare how different authors handle a specific element in their works. I especially like using children's books to study the author's craft because they are short enough that groups of students can make comparisons of various aspects of craft in a relatively short period of time (e.g., one class period). After the students examine various elements, bridge to asking them to use a similar technique as one of the writers they have studied. Ask students to select a piece of writing to specifically modify for improvements in the target area. When students examine how someone else uses language and then apply "lessons learned" to their own writing, dramatic improvements can result in writing as well as in reading.

Encourage students to play with words and think about word combinations by having a "We Like the Sound of This" bulletin board in the classroom. When students find word combinations or passages they like, have them copy the passage onto 3 × 5 cards or sticky notes, and post these on the special bulletin board for others to read. Be sure to ask each contributor to sign his or her contribution and put the source and page number of the quote on the card so that others who find the citation interesting can go to the original source if they wish. One way to ensure that your students are motivated to examine language and think about how it sounds is to award bonus points for citations placed on the special bulletin board.

It is critical that we get students thinking more deeply about what they read. Students must understand that there are many layers of text and of text understanding. Help your students understand that we read and reread a text to learn more about it and to think more deeply about various aspects of it. Text has multiple layers of meaning like the layers of an onion. While text is meant to be enjoyed, it is also good to understand that sometimes we want to pull it apart and look at it layer by layer. Like watching a movie again and again, each time we interact with the text, we find new elements that we had not seen before. We can read simply to appreciate and enjoy the text as the author intended, or we can read it to look at the words and the language. We can let it resonate with us and highlight special word combinations that are particularly meaningful. We can even try to understand why an author has chosen to write a particular text in the manner that he or she has. Encourage students to consider questions like these:

- "What impresses me about this author's writing or style?"
- "What elements of the author's craft make this writing interesting or give it a certain tone?"
- "What other books does this writing remind me of?"
- "What other authors have similar ideas or writing styles?"
- "How does this relate to other information or stories I already have read?"
- "How do different authors craft the same element such as creating imagery or creating suspense?"
- "What can I learn from this author that might help me in my own writing or to accomplish my own goals in life?"

Each time we reread a text, we develop new insights and additional perspectives that we did not have available to us before. This close examination from different perspectives gives us new levels of understanding that deepen meaning and the connections we have made with the text.

Learning to Summarize Text

Another skill relevant to student success on state assessments is being able to summarize text. Teach students to summarize and monitor their own comprehension by stopping to frequently paraphrase what they have read. Ask them, "Who can summarize the information we have learned up to this point?" or "Who can summarize for us what has just happened in this section of the story?" These stopping points help ensure that all students are following the text and comprehending the nuances that are taking place. It also helps build student capacity by modeling how to succinctly summarize small sections of text.

You can teach students to summarize the key points of an article directly by having students listen and follow along as you read a short article displayed on the overhead. After you have read the text to the students, shut off the projector and ask students to write down what they remember of the passage. Ask them to now work with a partner to write answers to the six key questions of "who, what, where, when, why, and how" from memory and from what they have jotted down after listening to you read. After students have discussed the key questions and written short answers to each one, ask them to use their answers to write an informative paragraph that will tell the gist of the article. If students seek details from the text, you can turn the overhead back on for a moment and allow students to verify any needed facts or information directly from the text. Keep the views brief, though, so students must rely on memory more than on the text. Remind students that they can add supporting details from the article, but they may not use more than a couple of words from any sentence directly in their own paragraph summary. Allow time for students to share their summaries and to discuss what elements were key components. Wormeli (2004) shares more strategies to help students in *Summarization in Any Subject: 50 Techniques to Improve Student Learning*.

Because state assessments require students to write their responses, spend as much time as possible asking students to write about anything and everything. The more students practice writing, the stronger they become as both readers and writers. Spend time showing students how to add, delete, and consolidate information in the texts they have written. Show students how to rearrange and edit text for redundant or irrelevant information and how to enhance the descriptors, adverbs, and adjectives in their written text. Teach struggling readers and second language learners how to recognize and use transition phrases and pronoun references in their work. Use sentence-combining exercises to help students think about how sentences sound when they are put together. Ask students to experiment with sentence combinations and reflect on "Which way sounds best?" Teach students how to write based on source materials and how to properly incorporate quotations and citations into the body of their writing. Students need deliberate minilessons and opportunities to practice these skills if they are to do well on similar tasks on state assessments.

Another excellent way to help students summarize longer stories or the plot of whole books is to have each student write 10 key details that happened in the story or book on 10 individual slips of paper. Once students have written their set of details, they compare what they have written to what a partner has written on his or her 10 slips of paper. Students read all 20 details and must come to consensus on the top 10 most important ideas. Details may be combined, reworded, or eliminated to get down to the new grouping of 10 main ideas. Once the pair has 10 agreed-on details, they meet with another pair who have also consolidated their own 20 slips down to 10 most important details. The foursome again consolidates, combines, or eliminates details until the group has once again reached consensus on 10 key details from the passage from the 20 slips the groups had when they combined. Once this new group of four arrives at agreement on the 10 most important details, together they write a paragraph or two that they feel summarizes the longer story or plot of the book. All of the groups share their writing with the class. After listening to all of the "gist" paragraphs, the class discusses which writing seems to capture the gist of the material most accurately and thoroughly. Not only does this activity help develop summary skills, but hearing the work of other students and groups also helps build student's writing and organization skills as well. The more students hear high-quality samples, the more their own work will improve.

Persuasive Essays Are Required in Some States

In some states, students are expected not only to write evaluative responses but also to demonstrate their skills in persuasive writing. Teach students how to plan a persuasive writing project by making notes, lists, or writing webs. Discuss how to develop a solid thesis statement that sets the tone for the work they will create. An example for elementary students might be as follows:

"Your brother wants a snake for a pet. Your mother is unsure about this being a good pet for your brother. Write a letter to your mother convincing her with details and facts that this either is or is not a good idea for your family."

Here's an example for a secondary student:

"The principal is considering having only one school dance per semester this year, but you think that having school dances is a fun part of the school social experience and that students should have monthly social opportunities. You are the student body president, and your friends expect you to get this problem solved. Write a persuasive essay to your principal to convince him to change his mind."

Once the essay is done, emphasize to students that since they want to be credible with the person to whom the work is addressed, they will have to ensure that their work is well edited for spelling, grammar, and punctuation. Ask students to critique each other's work and to provide suggestions on how the writer might strengthen his or her persuasive essay. Use rubrics to help students self-analyze their work. For secondary students, solicit the cooperation of the principal to read through the letters and place them into two piles based on the strength of the argument and presentation, marking each letter with either "Yes" or "Sorry." Read a few anonymous letters from each group to the class, and ask students to identify what features successful letters have and what differentiates successful from unsuccessful letters. Use the information students identify to make a classroom "recommendations" list and to develop a new persuasive letter that might go home to mom and dad asking for an increase in allowance or an additional privilege at home that the student would like. Before students take the letters home, ask them to again invite peers to critique the arguments and provide suggestions for revision based on the classroom guidelines for good persuasive writing. You should see some definite improvement in this task the second time around. It will be fun to see which letters get a supportive response from parents as well. Continue to practice persuasive writing any time that you can fit it into the schedule. Again, the more students practice, the better their performance at test time.

Using Solid Reading Techniques on a Daily Basis

The final way that students can become strategic and thinking readers is by our helping them focus on effective strategies before, during, and after reading. If students do not have the skills to process text deliberately and effectively, take the time to teach them specifically how to apply the various skills needed for each part of the reading task. Here are the key elements that students will need to practice for effective reading.

Before reading:

- Look over the text (titles, headings, charts, graphs, length, etc.).
- Understand what it is you want to learn or find out from the text.
- Look at how the material is organized or presented.
- Think about what you already know about the topic.
- Make some predictions about what you think the text will be about or what you want to know about the topic.

During reading:

- Continually ask, "Does this make sense? Do I understand what I just read?"
- Pay special attention to chapter titles, headings, subheadings, graphics, or pictures. Are words explained in the footnotes?
- Take notes, highlight, or use sticky notes to remind yourself about important information, to post questions, or to make connections to what you are reading.
- Whenever possible, try to visualize what is being described in your mind.
- Stop periodically to think about what you already know about the topic and how the new information links to this information. If you don't understand something, reread the text, make a note, talk with someone, or consult a resource such as a dictionary.

After reading:

- See if you met your purpose for reading.
- Summarize what you have read by jotting down a short paragraph of the key points or the gist of the text.
- Evaluate your notes and check for understanding. What was unclear for you? If you have questions, reread any sections that were not clear, or talk with someone who can help you answer your questions.
- Evaluate the ideas presented in the text, and think about connections that you can make from your own experiences or prior learning. What do you know from other texts that you have read, other classes, or your own experience that relates to this information? What connections can you make to this text?

• Review your notes and clarify in your notes any questions that may still be unanswered or need additional explanation.

• Find a way to think about or apply what you have learned in a new way so that the learning can be more meaningful. Ask, "What does this information mean for me either now or in the future?"

High-Performance Language Arts Instruction

If you want your students to perform well on state reading assessments, make sure that you thoroughly understand the performance expectations for your students. Help students think deeply about the text they are reading, and ask them for "proof" to justify their thoughts, ideas, and responses. Model throughout the year how to approach constructed-response tasks, and provide daily opportunities for students to practice the skills they will need to evaluate, analyze, synthesize, and justify their ideas and responses. Introduce them to self-analysis through rubrics, and prepare them to revise and improve their performance as they closely examine their own performance and ways to improve that performance. Use writing often to deepen learning and stretch thinking. When students practice their skills every day, they will be prepared for all types of assessments and will be able to demonstrate what they have learned and can do.

4 | Science

Science Becomes More Important

Under the No Child Left Behind Act (NCLB) of 2001, all states were required to establish science standards for every grade level by 2005 and to staff science classrooms with highly qualified teachers by the end of the 2005–06 school year. NCLB also called for states to develop and implement state science assessments and test students at least once a year in each of three grade spans: 3–5, 6–9, and 10–12 beginning in the 2007–08 school year. While many states originally adopted science standards in the 1990s, and some even tested student achievement in science, these standards were broad and not written to serve as guides for the development of grade-level assessments such as those required by NCLB. As such, many states have been working to revise their science standards so that they can better serve as the foundation for the new or revised assessments currently being developed to meet the testing implementation time line.

Criticism in recent years has suggested that the science standards currently in place in states are neither rigorous enough nor suited to producing students who think deeply and critically about scientific concepts. Stan Metzenberg (n.d.), a biology professor at California State University–Northridge and a member of the California state curriculum commission, wrote a scathing critique of current state science assessment efforts. He points to a collection of problems relating to science standards and current state science assessments. Some of the issues he cites include nonspecific state standards, too-low expectations for high school science performance, superficial assessment items that do not truly require an understanding of science concepts, and internal psychometric problems with item construction. Metzenberg also cites high instances on state assessments of what he calls "just in time teaching," where students are provided with enough text that they are able to answer a question based on reading the information provided in the test item rather than on a solid foundational understanding of the concepts of science. Metzenberg says, "When students do not need to think about science content to answer the questions the overall test result may be deceptive" (n.d., p. 2). He calls on states to refine state standards, raise the level of expectation for student performance, and develop assessments that truly measure knowing and doing science rather than simply surface-level content knowledge.

The past decade has also seen allegations that science instruction in the United States has been improperly taught as a discipline. According to geology professor Steven Schafersman (1991) of the University of Miami at Oxford, Ohio, science is often taught as simply a "fact-based" discipline in the United States rather than a process of approaching or discovering scientific concepts and principles:

> In retrospect, it seems obvious that when the information content of a discipline increases, it becomes even more vital to spend time, not learning more information, but learning methods to acquire, understand and evaluate this information and the great amount of new information that is not known now but will surely follow. Frankly, it is counterproductive to simply memorize and learn more new and isolated facts when future facts may eventually displace these. Thus, our science education policy has been completely backward, teaching more science facts and less scientific method rather than the converse. (p. 2)

In the past, relatively little research has been done on the best ways to teach science to students, but that may be changing soon. In late 2004, the National Research Council convened a 36-month study panel called the Board on Science Education whose mission is to examine the research on how science is best learned and taught. At the conclusion of the project, researchers hope to answer such questions as these: How is science learned? What are the critical stages in children's development of scientific concepts? Where might connections between lines of research need to be made? How does this help us understand how to teach science in K–8 classrooms? What other lines of research need to be pursued to make our understanding about how students learn science more complete? From this extensive and thorough analysis of the available research, the panel will prepare a comprehensive report that may set the stage for changes in the field of science instruction and assessment. The panel's report may well provide important information that will shape how science instruction will be taught in the future.

In addition, the national TIMSS Video Study (Roth et al., 2006) indicates that while American teachers have increased the number of hands-on activities being provided in U.S. classrooms as a result of recent training attempts in inquiry methods, content in science lessons is often secondary to classroom activities. From observational analysis, researchers concluded that teachers need to base their instruction on clearly specified science content learning goals and then select activities that support building coherent understandings of that conceptual goal. Teachers should carefully and thoughtfully develop just one or two science ideas that link together into a logical, coherent sequence. Students should be expected to demonstrate mastery of the concepts of science and should be able to support those concepts with specific evidence to demonstrate their understandings.

Researchers Roth and Garnier (2007) have outlined eight strategies that could help teachers create more focused and coherent lessons based on what they refer to as a "story line" approach. The steps are as follows:

1. Identify one main learning goal.

2. Communicate the purpose with goal statements and focus questions.

3. Select content representations that are matched to the learning goal.

4. Select activities that are matched to the learning goal.

5. Sequence the content story line.

6. Link content ideas and activities.

7. Highlight for students important ideas and links among them.

8. Summarize and synthesize important ideas.

While hands-on activities are important and clearly belong in the repertoire of U.S. science teachers, we must go beyond the superficial use of random activities that do not build solid, science concept knowledge. We must understand how to use a driving question to help students learn science ideas and concepts. Once we have identified the key learning goal, then we can develop important classroom activities that link student understandings. Combined with probing questions, opportunities for reflection, and discussions, students will be able to delve deeper into science concepts and understandings.

Promoting High-Quality Science Learning

In 2005, the Committee for Test Design for K–12 Science Achievement of the National Research Council published a report titled *Systems for State Science Assessment* (Wilson & Bertenthal, 2005). The committee outlined three definitions of science literacy: (1) knowledge of science content, (2) understanding science as a way of knowing, and (3) understanding and conducting scientific inquiry. The panel wrote, "A strong foundation of science content knowledge is a necessary component of the ability to think scientifically. The ability to plan a task, to notice patterns, to generate reasonable arguments and explanations, to draw analogies to other problems—all key elements of science literacy—are dependent on factual knowledge" (p. 39). They go on to say, however, that students are expected to understand scientific principles and be able to actively apply them rather than just simply absorb a set of facts, formulas, and procedures disconnected from a real-life context. They say that it is a student's capacity to integrate knowledge, skills, and procedures into new situations and tasks that truly is important. Students must learn "core principles" or "big ideas" in science as a source of coherence for their learning and content organization. Experts know how to apply their knowledge in the right situation, so it is important that students have multiple opportunities to use and apply the principles they are learning to promote thinking and transference to real-world contexts. "Helping students develop an understanding of when and how to use what they know is an important key to the development of scientific literacy" (p. 41). These ideas will form the basis for what states will use as the "core concepts" or what they expect students to know and be able to do in science. Once identified, these standards will be useful for making changes and revisions to state science content standards.

Thinking Deeply: Science as a Way of Knowing

In looking at science as a way of knowing, we know that all scientists, no matter what their field, have a common set of basic beliefs and attitudes about science. These foundational beliefs and attitudes must be communicated to students as well. For example, scientists believe that the world can be analyzed, observed, and explained. Scientists base their theories and interpretations on the premise that the world has order and that careful, systematic observation can provide important information. Scientists see consistency and durability with some ideas and accept that scientific views can change with verifiable evidence. They believe that scientific theories can explain what is observable and that current observations can help make connections to related phenomena as well as pave the way to make predictions about future events. Scientists believe that one approaches finding solutions to problems and questions in an organized and deliberate way. They believe that science is about continually testing the theories and revising as needed with verifiable proof, and this is what we must help our students understand.

We need to teach our students to *do* science in a coherent, thoughtful way rather than to just memorize science-related facts and information. They must use their knowledge of scientific concepts to reason, to make and justify predictions, and to conduct actual experiments that allow them to make observations and develop theories and explanations. Students must be taught to think deeply, to reflect, and to revise explanations in light of new or even contradictory information and observations. We should ask them to defend their ideas and hypotheses with solid evidence that supports their theories and conclusions. Students who can delve into scientific concepts and processes at this level can use their knowledge and understandings to think and to reason deeply about the world around them. These skills are what will enable our students to assume their place in the competitive world.

Doing Science: Science as Inquiry

One of the reasons that science has been harder to develop standards for than math or reading is that teaching science requires an agreement on core content or "big ideas" and an active, hands-on process. Authors of the National Research Council report (Wilson & Bertenthal, 2005) define scientific inquiry as "a set of skills and approaches that scientists use in conducting their work" (p. 42). They state that students should understand how scientific evidence is obtained as well as how scientific evidence is used to support explanations by scientists. They also recommend that before they graduate from high school, all students should have the opportunity to conduct a scientific investigation from start to finish. Students should experience identifying an important question, observing and analyzing data, generating explanations, organizing and presenting ideas and theories, and responding to criticism about the investigation process. A state standard that reflects an emphasis on inquiry as the foundation for science instruction might be written as follows:

> Students will develop inquiry skills to include analyzing, problem solving, and decision making by identifying pertinent questions and hypotheses, planning experiments and conducting trials, recording observations, analyzing data and creating interpretations, drawing and reporting conclusions, and summarizing results.

The skills that students will need to demonstrate mastery of scientific inquiry are developing hypotheses; conducting experiments and controlling variables; thinking critically; recording observational data; developing well-reasoned, logical theories and arguments; and coherently addressing criticism and arguments.

On state assessments, students may be asked to evaluate various aspects of an experiment, make evaluations and observations from the data, provide explanations or make predictions, or even critique the work that has been done. As states revise their science standards, many may include a performance component on their assessment. New York and Connecticut currently have a performance component in their state science assessments. The national K–12 science committee studying science reform states, "Science assessment that reflects the practices of science should focus not on the retention of discrete knowledge of facts or procedures but on assessing students' abilities to use scientific theories to explain phenomena, to make predictions in light of evidence, and to apply their science-related knowledge in approaching new and unfamiliar situations" (Wilson & Bertenthal, 2005, p. 50). As a result of recommendations like these, more states are also looking into incorporating a hands-on, performance component into their state assessment plans as the deadline for first testing students in 2007 looms.

New York's assessments will give us an idea of how performance assessment might be done in other states as well. In 2006, this assessment was given in grades 4 and 8 at the elementary level. The 4th grade students are given a two-part science exam that covers scientific knowledge, process, and performance. The first part of the assessment, which takes about an hour to complete, consists of multiple-choice and constructed-response questions around basic science concepts. The second part of the test measures how well students can perform scientific work by asking them to complete three small experiments. Working independently on each task, students have 15 minutes to visit each of the three stations in the classroom. While at each station, students conduct their experiment, record their information, and draw conclusions as required by the type of experiment they have been given. For teachers wanting more details, an example of New York's released items for the performance section of the test can be found at www.emsc.nysed.gov/osa/. Examining the assessment sample can help us learn more about what might be expected of students on the science performance assessments that other states may develop in the near future. (Appendix A contains additional links to state assessments currently in place around the United States.)

Let's also examine the 8th grade science assessment to see how this test is conducted. When students enter the testing area, teachers have the materials in place and ask students to sit at one station and to perform each task by themselves. After each 15-minute task, students rotate to the next station and complete the work at that station until they have visited all three stations. Each station is a unique and independent experiment that tests various skills and abilities in science. At station 1, for example, students might be asked to roll a ball down a ramp and observe how it moves a plastic cup at the end of the ramp. The student is asked to think about what variables influence how far the cup moves when the ball hits it. Students might then be expected to design an experiment, record observations, and formulate a hypothesis for this task. At station 2, the students might be asked to observe the properties of soap bubbles and predict how they would behave if placed in water. Students would be asked to observe, conduct the experiment, and measure such properties as mass, volume, and density of the two samples. At station 3, the students might be asked to prepare cells for viewing, use a microscope to observe the cells, and then draw what they see under both low and high power. Teachers are provided with rubrics and work in teams to ensure that student responses are accurately recorded for each section of the performance test. Sample performance anchor papers ensure that teachers have samples to use as comparisons when determining the number of points to give each response.

Changes in the Science Classroom

In light of these recommended changes in science instruction, what should teachers do to help students successfully demonstrate their knowledge of science content? First, we need to help students understand that it is vital to blend what is already known with new observations and learning. We can help students understand that science is a dynamic field that is always open to revision as more information becomes known.

Second, we must help students develop skills in the areas of observing data, developing hypotheses, controlling variables and conducting appropriate experiments, and thinking critically about the phenomena they observe in the real world. In other words, we must teach science by actively involving students in hands-on learning and experimentation. This type of deep learning cannot come from just the pages of a book.

Finally, we must help our students learn to self-assess their work so that science becomes as much about the process as about the outcome or result. Students must also be taught how to create plausible theories and how to develop cohesive and well-reasoned arguments to support their theories and experimental designs. When we do these things, we will truly be developing students who think deeply and analytically about science.

What Might Science Assessment Look Like?

Even though changes in how science is assessed may soon be on the horizon, in all probability, multiple-choice and constructed-response items will still appear on state tests, at least for the foreseeable future. Let's examine the format that these items currently take around the United States so that we can better understand how to prepare our students for the assessments that may soon be coming down the pike in states that have not yet implemented a science assessment program.

Typical science assessments ask students to provide information about the properties of systems, the structure of various systems, or the changes that take place in systems. For example, students might be asked to identify the correct sequence in a cycle or to name the parts of a specific item. Often, they must choose the "best explanation" for something or to analyze whether an experiment is appropriately set up as described. Students might be asked to evaluate the likely success of an experiment, identify dependent and independent variables, predict a missing value, describe a trend by looking at provided data, or even suggest possible reasons for an observed change. They might also be asked to describe the relationship between two things or to predict how X would be affected by a specific change in Y. Finally, students might be asked to identify or describe a process or determine what factors affect a specific process. Any released items from your state assessment will help you identify which types of questions are likely to appear on the multiple-choice sections that may be incorporated into your state assessment instruments.

Here are some examples of questions found on state science assessments:

Elementary Examples:

• The chart above shows the characteristics of four different habitats. In which habitat would a lizard be found? List three details that support your decision.
  • Which diagram above shows an example of metamorphosis?
  • Using the classification chart below, classify all of the items shown above into two different groups, according to a feature that one group has and that the other group does not have. Write the feature on the line at the top of each column and add the names of the items to each box under the appropriate column.
  • Examine the chart of average temperatures for a week in Seattle, Washington. Based on what you see in the chart, predict a reasonable temperature for the missing data from the four choices given.
  • Look at the sequence of pictures above. Which phase of the moon would come next in the sequence shown?

Secondary Examples:

• The graph shows how the momentum of a given mass changes during motion. According to the information provided, what is the momentum in kg m/s at 2.75 seconds? Justify your answer.
  • Which wave above shows the wave with the greatest amplitude and why?
  • Which of the graphs shown best illustrates the relationship between frequency and the effective range of the sound wave described in the passage? Explain the relationship.
  • Which configuration of pulleys and belts shown will result in the fastest rotation of spindle 2? Explain your response.

Constructed-response items might ask students to think about a specific concept and then create a response to analyze that concept. For example, a constructed-response question at the elementary level might ask students to identify similarities and differences between the life cycle of a butterfly and the life cycle of a grasshopper. A secondary student might be asked to compare how concentrations of various chemical compounds found in a pond might manifest themselves in different types of fish. In other types of questions, students may need to identify and explain a process that is described or to explain the factors affecting the process. For example, they might be asked to explain how the forces of kinetic energy work on a bouncing ball. A constructed-response question might even take things a step further by asking students to compare the life cycle of a newborn human with the life cycle of another species and to explain the thinking behind their comparisons. In other examples, students may be asked to explain a natural cycle or how something functions, such as the cycle of rain or photosynthesis. Students may be presented with a text and a scientifically related dilemma such as the following: "Should people be required to spay or neuter their pets? Use examples and illustrations from the text to support your opinion." Constructed-response tests often ask students to read an informational passage, analyze it, and then draw and support a conclusion. For example, "Would a snake make a good pet? Give details from the text to support your opinion." In each case, students will need to be well trained in sorting, classifying, analyzing, and writing about the information they have received. Teachers who use similar procedures during ongoing instruction and require their students to process learning at the "Why?" or "How do you know?" level produce students who have no difficulty responding to state assessment questions of a similar nature.

Some ways that we can help students organize and process data more deeply are by asking them to make comparisons of all types. Help them define, classify, and sort information and attributes so that they are comfortable seeing differences and similarities in their environment. Help them make comparisons and organize data with helpful graphic organizers that make data easy to see and to evaluate. Drawing comparisons and making conclusions are essential skills for scientific learning. Students evaluate and learn to analyze information by actively participating in such activities. Here are some examples of constructed-response items that ask students to use these skills:

Elementary: "Use a Venn diagram to show the differences between an alligator and a crocodile."
Elementary: "How is a marsupial different from a mammal?"

Secondary: "Describe several challenges that scientists face when trying to find out about volcanoes. Explain how technology can help them overcome these difficulties, and draw any diagrams that may be needed to clarify your response."

Secondary: "Early scientists classified sponges in the Plant Kingdom, but scientists now place them in the Animal Kingdom. Discuss at least two characteristics that might justify placing the sponge in each category. Which do you believe is more correct and why?"

On many state assessments, students are asked to think about a specific text provided on the test. They are then asked to use this information to respond in various ways. Helping students learn how to select the important information from a text and summarize it is important in all disciplines.

Here is a fun way to get students to read the material, talk about their understandings, and also summarize the information. Select a section of text that can easily be divided into three to five parts. Assign students to groups based on the number of parts of the text, and ask each student to read a specific section of the text for his or her group. Each student will only read one section of the text selection. As they read, students make notes to answer the question "What is the most important information that someone would need from this part of the text?" When students have finished reading their own section of the text, they then share, in order, the information they have identified and the notes they have made. While listening, each student should make his or her own notes and ask any questions about the material. Students should be encouraged to go back to the text to clarify any questions or misunderstandings that may come up. When all students have shared what they believe to be the key points of their sections, the groups summarize the major points that they understand from the material. This summary can either be discussed as a class or be completed in written form. Not only will students enjoy sharing and talking about the material, but it will be easy for you to detect any misunderstandings that need to be corrected.

Introduce students to rubrics, and teach them how to self-evaluate their work. Even young students can self-evaluate if given rubrics that are written in age-appropriate, "kid-friendly" terms. Once students are comfortable using rubrics, you can even ask them to help you develop the rubrics that will be used to evaluate their hands-on learning projects. Montgomery County Public Schools (2002) in Rockville, Maryland, has an excellent sample of a Constructed-Response Science Rubric that might give you ideas for how you can use rubrics in your own classroom. Rubrics help students learn to shape and analyze new aspects of their work that will prove beneficial over and over again.

Although textbooks can be useful and excellent collections of factual information, they are often not the most current or interesting sources of information on the topics that you need to help your students understand. In addition to textbook information, regularly provide current, age-appropriate scientific articles or newspaper articles about scientific events, discoveries, or theories that are called for in your state standards. Ask students to read the articles, exploring how the information relates to what they already know or to what is provided in the textbook. Ask students to explain their thinking and responses as they discuss their opinions or ideas. Try to link learning to real-world concepts that students already care about and have experienced. For example, instead of presenting a dry textbook account of Newton's laws of motion, you might provide information about seat belts and accident safety reports, and then ask students to determine if they think that states should have mandatory seat belt laws. Ask students to discover the connections themselves whenever possible so that learning is deeper and more meaningful.

Another example of connecting real-life learning to what students know and care about might be the following: instead of learning about arteries from a textbook, ask students to build an artificial artery. Provide lots of graphs, charts, and data sources for students to examine and analyze. Think about the terms that students are responsible for knowing. How can we make these terms memorable and meaningful to students? It is guaranteed that students who must find out how an artery works and then create their own artificial one will understand the concepts far deeper than those students who only read about it in their textbooks.

Outstanding Web sites invite students to participate in simulations, find and analyze real data, and even conduct scientific research alongside real scientists. Appendix B includes a very small sample of some of these great resources. In addition, a book that I find very helpful is Barry Young's (1996) *Free Stuff for Science Buffs*. This book is a treasure trove of Web sites and sources of free materials that every science teacher will find very useful to expand and deepen student learning. Finding ways to make learning meaningful and relevant to students will enable your classroom to be an exciting, vibrant place where students will be better able to think deeply, thoroughly, and abstractly.

Getting Ready for Change

Understanding how science assessment is likely to change over the coming decade will help us prepare for any instructional challenges that may lie ahead in science. Students will be expected to actively apply scientific information rather than just absorb facts and information in isolation. We will need to help our students develop general knowledge about science content; an understanding of science as a way of knowing and understanding; and the ability to use scientific inquiry to test theories, examine the world, and conduct meaningful scientific inquiry. The key words that might influence science instruction are *explain, analyze, justify, predict, compare,* and *support.* When we help students understand the "big ideas" and interrelationships in the world of science, they will be able to truly approach the world in an analytical and organized manner.

5 Social Studies

When professional organizations were coming together to standardize curricular content in the early 1990s, the National Council for the Social Studies put forth its own set of standards in 1994. These standards, organized around 10 thematic topics, include everything from culture to history to citizenship. They set forth what the professional organization defines as the content "worth knowing" for the social studies discipline. Individual states examined these standards and developed their own sets of content standards, so what is taught under the social studies umbrella varies widely from state to state. Because content standards across the nation can include content from state, U.S., or world history; geography; economics; or civics as part of the curriculum, it is vital that social studies teachers closely study the standards and content scope of their own state for the grade level they teach.

Social Studies Achievement Is Sampled at the Federal Level

Although social studies is not yet a part of the content areas that NCLB requires states to test for student academic performance, student achievement at the federal level has been randomly sampled every few years since the late 1960s. The federal National Assessment for Educational Progress (NAEP) civics test was first administered in 1969 to sample student academic performance in this area and has been administered five times since that date to elementary school children and three times to high school seniors. The most recent administration was in March 2006, with the results for civics, economics, geography, U.S. history, and world history available at http://nces.gov/nationsreportcard/subjectareas.asp. To understand the national priorities and values in this content area, we can examine what content is covered in the NAEP assessments.

The NAEP civics test covers five fundamental questions that developers feel outline ideas and information essential to citizens' comprehension of democracy in the United States:

1. What are civic life, politics, and government?

2. What are the foundations of the American political system?

3. How does the government established by the Constitution embody the purposes, values, and principles of American democracy?

4. What is the relationship of the United States to other nations and to world affairs?

5. What are the roles of citizens in American democracy?

In addition to civics, the NAEP also periodically samples the content mastery of students in the areas of U.S. history, economics, geography, and world history. The NAEP social studies battery is designed around four themes:

• Change and Continuity in American Democracy: Ideas, Institutions, Practices, and Controversies

• Gathering and Interactions of Peoples, Cultures, and Ideas

• Economic and Technological Changes and Their Relation to Society, Ideas, and the Environment

• Changing Role of America in the World

The NAEP uses eight chronological periods to measure the major areas of U.S. history: America's Beginnings (to 1607), Colonization and Settlement (1607–1763), Revolution and the Birth of the Nation (1763–1815), Expansion and Reform (1801–61), Civil War and Reconstruction (1850–77), Industrialization (1865–1920), World Wars (1914–45), and Contemporary America (1945–present). Students are assessed in two cognitive dimensions. The first is historical knowledge, which includes knowing and understanding people, events, concepts, themes, movements, and historical sources. The second is relationships, patterns, and connections, which require a much deeper level of understanding and analysis.

NAEP assessments include multiple-choice test items as well as detailed constructed-response questions that require complex responses. The constructed-response sections assess deeper thinking. Students must to be able to sequence events, recognize multiple perspectives, understand an era through the eyes of various groups, and have a general understanding of U.S. history as a whole. Constructed-response assessments also require extensive use of higher-order thinking and processing skills. Students are expected to analyze and interpret various historical events, including explaining issues, identifying historical patterns, establishing cause-and-effect relationships, finding value statements, establishing significance, applying historical knowledge, weighing evidence to draw sound conclusions, making defensible generalizations, and rendering insightful accounts of the past. Clearly, students must have a complex and thorough understanding of the underlying concepts of social studies and be able to apply those skills to deep levels to demonstrate what they know and can do in this content area.

Testing Student Performance in Social Studies at the State Level

Although the No Child Left Behind Act of 2001 did not yet mandate that states assess student performance in social studies, several states have developed and do administer annual assessments of various types to measure student learning in some aspect of social studies. For some states, assessment mainly takes place in civics; in other states, students are also tested on their understandings of historical events and geography.

Just as in the other content areas, most states currently use a blend of multiple-choice items and constructed-response items to test student performance. A few states have incorporated assessment sections that ask students to review and analyze actual primary source historical documents and interpret their meaning. Some states only test in one area (e.g., civics), while other states have very broad and comprehensive assessment programs in place. In New York State, for example, students must know and understand concepts in state history, U.S. and world history, geographic land features, economics, civics, citizenship, and government. The state assessment instrument is made up of 50 percent multiple-choice items, 20 percent constructed-response items, and 30 percent primary source documents questions. On the document-based portion, 10 percent of the questions consist of multiple-choice questions, and the remaining 20 percent requires students to compose an original essay. Examples of this assessment can be found at the New York Department of Education Web site: www.emsc.nysed.gov/osa/elintsocst.html.

By contrast, students in Texas are given a multiple-choice test based on five standards: demonstrating understanding of issues and events in U.S. history, understanding geographic influences on issues and events in U.S. history, recognizing economic and social influences on U.S. history, recognizing political influences on U.S. history, and using critical thinking skills to analyze social studies information. Students must demonstrate understanding of key issues and events affecting the United States from colonization through the Civil War and must be able to read maps; interpret political cartoons; understand time lines of key events; fill in missing information in charts and diagrams; and compare and contrast information, events, and theories. Samples can be seen at the following Web sites: www.tea.state.tx.us/student.assessment/resources/online/2003/grade8/socialstudies.htm for the 8th grade assessment sample and www.tea.state.tx.us/student.assessment/resources/online/2003/grade10/socialstudies.htm for the 10th grade assessment sample.

If your state does administer a social studies assessment, check Appendix A for a Web site that might provide sample released items and describe which standards are assessed, how they are assessed, and the areas of emphasis. The more you know about how your state assessment aligns with your state content standards, the better able you will be to prepare your students for success.

Lesson Ideas to Strengthen Skills

Most social studies assessment questions are designed around a specific stimulus that students use to respond to the question. Some examples of stimulus items are graphs, charts, maps, time lines, graphic organizers, political cartoons or slogans, and photographs or pictographs. For this reason, the wise teacher ensures that students have frequent opportunities not only to analyze and interpret these items but to actually create them in a meaningful context as well. Let's take a look at how we might enhance our lessons to strengthen student skills in reading and interpreting these various items.

Charts and Graphs

Considering graphs and charts first, I find *USA Today* to be one of my favorite sources for appealing, helpful graphs and charts to use in the classroom. This newspaper presents information in ways that are colorful, easy to read, and designed around contemporary topics. Clip out interesting graphs and charts, and use them to help students become comfortable reading and interpreting them on a regular basis. Enlarge and copy them onto an overhead transparency to use in the classroom. Model reading the information and drawing conclusions about the topics and information presented. Students will quickly get the hang of reading and interpreting the data that these graphs and charts contain so that when presented with similar tasks on assessments, they will be very comfortable analyzing similar information.

While understanding how to read graphs and charts is helpful, actually creating them moves the activity to an even deeper level of thinking. Students begin to understand them more thoroughly and can apply the information in new ways. The Internet can be a helpful source of great lesson plans appropriate for creating graphs and charts of all types. One Web site that I particularly like is the Population Reference Bureau site at www.prb.org. On the Educator tab, you will find several outstanding lesson plans where students of all ages can explore data and create their own graphs and charts using current population data. An excellent one for middle or high school students is the Sport Franchise unit, which examines U.S. population changes in relation to the growth of Major League Baseball. Appendix B also contains a small sampling of some interesting and helpful activities, simulations, and "virtual field trips" that will help you integrate hands-on activities into your social studies classroom.

Time Lines

Next, let's consider how we might use time lines in our classroom. Several state tests ask students to place key historical figures or historical events into their proper sequence. In my experience, students often lack a sense of time and sequence with regard to history. Helping students pinpoint events and happenings on a classroom time line can ground their thinking and help them have a better sense of historical flow. A room-sized time line where students plot historical events as they are studied over the course of the school year visually represents how people and events are sequenced over time.

Make time lines personal by asking students to create their own "historical time line" of key events that have taken place both in the world and in their own lives during their lifetime. Ask students to interview parents or grandparents to get a sense of the world events that have happened in their lifetimes. This activity makes for an interesting classroom discussion and real-life historical record.

Tools to Better Read Textbooks

As most social studies teachers will readily admit, social studies textbooks are notoriously concept-dense and problematic for students to read and understand. An excellent way to help students find ways to simplify and organize the information is to teach them to use graphic organizers. The Internet includes many sources for ideas for graphic organizers, but one site that I particularly like is www.readingquest.org, which has both graphic organizers and active learning strategies specifically for social studies teachers. Using graphic organizers to simplify and organize complex materials helps students better understand the information and be able to connect to it in more concrete ways. For example, while studying the Revolutionary War, you might have students create a compare/contrast chart to describe the viewpoints of the Loyalists and the Patriots in colonial America. For the Civil War, students might compare and contrast the strengths and weaknesses of Yankee versus Rebel troops. A chart such as the one in Figure 5.1 can help students clarify and simplify complex thinking around the viewpoints of historical time periods. Allow students time to think and reflect as a group so that all students can contribute to the thinking process in active ways.

FIGURE 5.1
Social Studies Topic Comparison Chart

	Strengths	**Weaknesses**
Yankee Troops		
Rebel Troops		

Another way that social studies teachers can help students understand how to process concept-dense material is by using the "think-aloud" strategy. Read a particularly difficult section of text aloud for students, and think out loud about the problems readers encounter as they read the text. Reflecting out loud will show your students how you monitor your own understanding of the material and what you do to ensure that you understand what you are reading. For example, you might say, "Let's see, from the title, I predict that this section of the text is going to tell me about . . . , and I can see from the bold headings in this section that I will be learning about a, b, and c." As you read, describe anything that you picture in your mind or any connections to what you already know that you might be making. Whenever possible, make analogies such as "This reminds me of . . ." or "This makes me think of. . . ." Be sure to stop at complex or potentially confusing points to demonstrate "fix-up" strategies that you use to monitor ongoing comprehension. For example, you might say, "Let's see, that didn't make sense. Maybe I had better slow down and read that again"; or "I'm not sure if I understand this yet, but I will read on a little further to see if it gets a bit clearer to me. If not, I might have to go back and reread that section to see if I can understand it better." Following your demonstration, ask students to summarize what you did and why it was a helpful strategy to use while reading complex text. If most of the students seem to need help processing the text, you may also want to have students take turns talking through a dense text with a partner until they become comfortable reading text in this content area.

Political Cartoons

Political cartoons are a fun way to help students learn to make inferences and link their background knowledge to contemporary issues. You can find a large collection of political cartoons as well as good teaching ideas at the Web site of political cartoonist Daryl Cagle: http://cagle.msnbc.com/politicalcartoons. Again, model how to interpret a political cartoon by using the think-aloud strategy until students understand how to approach the task. Allow students to work in groups to interpret political cartoons so they can share information and background knowledge.

When teaching students how to examine and interpret political cartoons, ask small groups to consider the following questions as they examine a political cartoon:

1. What is the title or cartoon caption? What do you know about this topic?

2. Are there any important dates or numbers in the cartoon? Any bold or enlarged words?

3. Who are the people pictured, and what key words or phrases do you see?

4. What words or phrases seem to be significant? What clues make you think they are important?

5. What emotions are shown in the cartoon? How do you know?

6. What is happening in the cartoon?

7. What is the message of the cartoon?

8. Who would agree and who would disagree with the message of the cartoon? Why would they agree or disagree?

A good follow-up activity would be to have students write about their own thoughts and feelings about the commentary in the political cartoon they examined. In addition to the questions just listed, possible topics for a one- to two-page essay include "Would you find living in X Country enjoyable?" or "Would you have enjoyed living during the time when X happened?" Remind students to use examples from the textbook to support their position.

You can use similar procedures with historical posters and slogan signs. Ask students to carefully identify the elements so that they can break down the information and make the appropriate connections and interpretations.

Historical Photographs

Several state social studies assessments ask students to draw conclusions and make connections based on the information they see in a historical photo. Again, a plethora of Web sites provide historical photos to use with students. An interesting and helpful government site that shows agricultural life from 1937 to 1943 is at www.usda.gov/oc/photo/histfeat.htm. A Civil War collection of images is located at www.treasurenet.com/images, and pictures about Pearl Harbor are available at http://gohawaii.about.com/cs/photogalleries/a/pearl_photos.htm. These are just a few of the great Web sites where you can find historical photos perfect for use in the classroom.

Ask your students to describe what is happening in the photo, identify any people, and describe what the photo tells them about life during this time frame or historical era. Students could also write about whether they would have liked to have lived during this time period and what challenges or benefits there might have been for people living then. Here are some typical questions on state assessments with regard to pictures:

- "Which statement best describes the events of the picture shown?"
- "Give two examples from the picture that show. . . ."

• "Using clues provided by the picture, discuss how life was different for children during the industrial period of American history than for children today."

Help students become comfortable analyzing photographs with partners or in small groups. Ask them to answer the following questions:

1. Who is pictured in the photo, and what activities are going on?
2. What details might provide clues as to the time frame of this picture?
3. What are some things that you can infer from this photo?
4. What was life like in this historical period? What might be some of the problems or situations that people faced during this period?
5. What do you wonder about this time period? What would you like to know more about?

When students have discussed the photo and jotted down some answers to these questions, have them share their picture and thoughts with another pair or small group. Can the second group bring any additional insights to examining the photo and the same set of questions? This "second pass" helps students think more deeply about the content and the connections they have made.

On many state assessments, students are presented with a short descriptive passage that describes a person, historical event, or concept. Students are asked to examine the information and then draw a conclusion, make a connection, or provide an explanation based on this material. While it is impossible to anticipate exactly what material may be selected for inquiry, this information will most likely be drawn from the standards that students are expected to master for that course or grade level. Again, analyzing any released items will help you identify the format and ways that questions are presented. Analyze any vocabulary terms that students will be expected to know and use. Be sure students clearly understand and can use the appropriate terminology in their responses as well. With this information, you will be better prepared to provide similar experiences to your students throughout the school year.

Helping Students with Social Studies Constructed-Response Questions

While some states do ask students to respond to short-answer questions such as "Give two advantages the Erie Canal provided for transporting goods in America" or "Discuss two ways that life changed for slaves when they became sharecroppers," several states ask students to write a longer thematic essay about a particular social studies topic. Although they are similar to traditional essays, which were covered in Chapter 2, thematic essays have a few unique characteristics.

Thematic essays are based on a specific theme commonly discussed in the social sciences. These themes might cover topics like change, diversity, interdependence, nationalism, urbanization, physical systems, environment, scarcity, belief systems, citizenship, power, or human rights. Students may be asked to define the term and then provide historical examples of this theme. They may also be asked to connect their understandings to a concept or process to explain, justify, or provide support for their own opinion on the topic. For example, while writing on an environment theme, students might be asked to discuss the term, cite examples of environmental concerns, and then discuss how each person might be able to effect positive change in his or her own local environment.

Teaching students to think globally and analytically is a complex task. The following activity might help students examine how different people can view the same issues differently: Ask students to think about how the news media shape our perceptions about world events. Brainstorm with the class topics that are currently in the news. Have students break out into groups. Each group should choose one of the topics to track and research in more detail. Provide a variety of daily newspapers, and allow time for students to look through each set of newspapers for their topics. When they locate an article, they should cut it out and tape it to a piece of paper, labeling each article with its source, date, and page. If students spot articles for another group, they can also gather these and pass them along to the appropriate group to save time. Try to gather as many articles as possible on the topic for a few weeks. Each group should have 15–20 articles on their topic.

Arrange the articles chronologically by newspaper source. As they gather the articles, ask students to read each of their articles carefully and discuss the writer's point of view for each one. Place their observations on sticky notes, and attach them to each article for reference.

At the end of the gathering period, ask students to review their articles and the notes they have made. How have the authors' viewpoints changed over the time they began writing? How do they feel about the issue? Do other writers from other sources agree with their viewpoint? Do different papers perceive this issue differently? How can you tell? Ask students to develop a position paper for the prompt "Do journalists influence how we perceive world events? Use examples and illustrations from the information you have gathered to support your team's position in a two- to three-page essay."

Another version of this activity that can help students think more deeply about a historical period or event is to find two versions of the same era or event that present very different accounts. For example, ask students to look at historical documents from the time of the Japanese internment during World War II and then contrast this information with a diary account of these same internment camps. Again, the Internet is a rich source of alternative points of view on this historical topic. After reading several accounts, ask students to discuss why historical accounts of the same event differ so radically. These types of discussions can then lead to having students look at more contemporary issues from multiple perspectives as well. Which groups benefit, and which might not? What countries benefit from various policies and political philosophies? These topics can lead students into deep thinking and rich discussion.

In addition to providing classroom instruction that encourages students to look at thematic strands, help students assess their own thematic essays. When students self-analyze, they form stronger insights into how they can improve and strengthen their own work from the "inside out." Begin by demonstrating to students how to analyze various essays, and then ask students to work in partners to analyze their own work. Help students learn to construct clear, concise, and relevant responses that communicate their ideas. Model for students: "How do I approach this task? What am I supposed to do?"

Help students identify key words in the prompt such as *explain, describe,* or *compare and contrast.* Remind students to always include information that shows the "proof" for points they are making in their essay. Is the flow logical, and does their position make sense? Use the rubric provided by your state if it has administered a state thematic essay question, or use the sample in Figure 5.2 as a starting point to help students analyze and improve their own work.

Using Primary Documents to Teach Social Studies

In addition to multiple-choice or thematic essay questions, some states ask students to demonstrate understandings and deep thinking by reading primary source materials such as official documents, newspaper articles, maps, diary or journal entries, letters, invitations, and other such original artifacts. Help students understand that primary and secondary source materials help historians put together clues about what life was really like during historical periods from various perspectives. Together these artifacts and documents make up the historical record of generations who have come before us. Remind students that published documents are not necessarily true, accurate, or reliable just because they have been published. All creators have a point of view and bias that will be reflected in the documents they leave behind. By reading and examining primary and secondary source documents, students can identify pressing questions, make inferences and interpretations, draw conclusions, and critically analyze the information they find. When students analyze information at this level, they are operating in the realm of a true social scientist.

State assessments typically provide students with a related group of documents on the same topic or historical event and then ask them to draw conclusions and make interpretations about some aspect of it—such as how people felt about it or what they did to solve a particular problem. For example, students might be provided with several documents about the Civil War and be asked to respond to a task prompt like this one:

FIGURE 5.2
Generic Social Studies Thematic Essay Scoring Rubric

5 Points
- Essay shows a clear and comprehensive understanding of the theme.
- Essay addresses all parts of the task prompt.
- Essay is well written, is easy to read, and flows logically.
- Essay contains rich details, facts, and examples for key points.
- Essay includes a strong introduction, logical arrangement of arguments, and a summary of key points.

4 Points
- Essay shows an understanding of the theme and provides a definition.
- Essay addresses most aspects of the task prompt.
- Essay is well written but may be less developed or have minor technical problems that do not impede the logical flow of the arguments.
- Theme is supported with accurate facts, details, and examples but is less well developed or complete than a 5-point essay.
- Essay has a good introduction and conclusion.

3 Points
- Essay shows some comprehension of the theme and an acceptable definition.
- Essay may fail to address all aspects of the task prompt.
- Essay is coherent with some level of detail but lacks depth.
- Theme may be presented with some factual errors and lack of detail.
- Theme is present in introduction but may have weak concluding statements.

2 Points
- Student demonstrates limited understanding of the theme and uses vague or inaccurate information in the response.
- Essay does not adequately analyze the theme or incorrectly analyzes the theme.
- Essay lacks a coherent focus and may go off on tangents or provide a very limited focus.
- Essay may have several factual errors, some of which seriously hamper understanding.
- Essay may be poorly written with many organizational, grammatical, or mechanical errors that impede reader comprehension.

1 Point
- Essay shows limited understanding of the theme.
- Essay has no logical sequence and may go off on unrelated tangents.
- Essay omits concrete examples, and details are weak or nonexistent.
- Severe organizational, grammatical, or mechanical errors make the essay difficult to follow in a logical manner.

Read documents 1–10 carefully. Write an essay about how the Civil War pitted brother against brother and the difficulties it caused families in both the North and the South. In your essay, discuss how families handled the conflict and how they dealt with the scars and aftermath of war when it was over. You will have 90 minutes to construct your essay on this topic.

Sometimes the document-based section of the test can also have short-answer constructed-response questions such as "List three examples of hardships the Rebel soldiers faced during the war" or "Describe the attitude toward the Civil War demonstrated by the soldiers' families in both the North and the South. How did they differ?"

The documents or passages on state assessments are designed to measure students' ability to make a logical inference, analyze information, or synthesize information into a logical, cogent response. Some questions require using information found at the literal level, while others require a deeper understanding and handling of more implicitly stated ideas and connections. In other words, students have to read text, analyze or synthesize what they have read, and then produce a response based on this thinking. Questions are constructed so that students must apply several different skills to complete the acts of comprehending, interpreting, and evaluating various aspects of text.

Using primary source documents in the classroom can help students apply concepts they are learning and can extend their thoughts and ideas in more authentic ways. They can also help teachers evaluate whether students have mastered certain skills and concepts. The Internet has many outstanding sources of primary documents and journal source documents that can easily serve as the centerpiece of student activities. More extensive information about incorporating primary and secondary source documents into your teaching can be found at www.edteck.com or at the Web site of social studies expert Peter Pappas: www.peterpappas.com. Appendix B also has some good examples of open-ended activities and virtual field trip sites that can provide students with outstanding examples of primary and secondary source documents.

Using State Standards to Guide Curriculum

To identify what vocabulary your students might encounter on state social studies assessments, first make a list of the topics for which they are responsible from state standards. For example, here are the state content expectations from the state of Washington for U.S. history.

US1.2.1: Describe and compare patterns of life over time in the following historical periods:
- "Indian" cultures (prehistory to 1492)
- Worlds Meet: Western Europe, West Africa, the Americas
- Settlement and Colonization (1607-1776)
- Revolution and Constitution (1754-1789)
- U.S. Expansion (1776-1850)

US1.2.2: Identify and analyze major issues, people, and events in U.S. history from the Revolution to 1900 including:
- Revolution, Constitution, and New Nation (1763-1820)
- Expansion and Reform (1801-1861)
- Civil War and Reconstruction (1850-1877)
- Industrialization, Immigration, Urbanization (1870-1900)

US1.2.3: Identify and analyze major concepts, people, and events in 20th century U.S. History including:
- Emergence of America as a world power (1890-1918)
- Reform, prosperity, and depression
- WW II, the Cold War, and International Relations (1939-Present)
- Post-World War II domestic, political, social, and economic issues (1945-present)

Taking just the topic of the Civil War and Reconstruction from the list above, a quick scan of the content material will reveal that some vocabulary words that it would be important for students to be able to define, as well as understand and use the principal or concept, might include the following:

Confederacy	Rebel	secede	emancipation
Yankee	abolition	fugitive	opposition
servitude	compromise	cavalry	anesthesia
Union	Gettysburg Address	tourniquet	infantry

The standards and the released items will also be helpful for lesson planning. For example, the state of New York Social Studies Standard 1 says, "Students will use a variety of intellectual skills to demonstrate their understanding of major ideas, eras, themes, developments, and turning points in the history of the United States and New York." This standard is broad and provides an expectation that students will need to use a variety of higher-order processing skills to show their understanding of the history of the United States and the state of New York. Again, this suggests a very large content base. Let's narrow that content field by further exploring the released assessments provided at www.nysedregents.org/testing/scostei/gr8bk1606.pdf for the 8th grade. While this list is not all-inclusive, examining the content of the state-released item assessment shows us that students will be expected to have extensive understandings of the following ideas, eras, themes, developments, and turning points:

1. How do we use archaeology to understand a culture and people (Aztecs, Incas, and Mayans, for example) even if they have disappeared?

2. Who colonized North America? What were the effects? What problems did they face? What were the political issues, and how were they resolved?

3. How did the colonies become united? What problems or issues did they face, and what key events and political events influenced this time period?

4. How was a new government established? What were the problems, concerns, or political issues? What documents were important and why?

5. How did the new government operate, and why was it formed that way?

6. How did the country expand, and what were the problems and issues associated with expansion?

7. What economic and political events led to the Civil War, and how did it impact the country? What were the key issues and events leading up to, during, and following the war?

8. What key judicial cases influenced American life and politics? What key documents, policies, or new laws changed life in America?

9. How did the Industrial Revolution change life in America both socially and politically? How did corporations influence economics or government? How did the United States interact with the world socially, politically, or economically?

10. How did the United States become involved in World War I and World War II, and what were the social, political, and economic issues of these time periods?

11. What was the "Cold War," and what were the social, political, and economic issues of this time period?

12. What were the issues behind the Civil Rights movement, and how did it influence life, economics, and politics in the United States?

13. What benefits, problems, or issues has industrialization generated for the United States or the world socially, economically, or politically?

While the specific questions may change from year to year, generally test makers use the same basic concepts when designing test items. When organizing my teaching for the school year, I would want to make sure that my students had solid understandings of these key topics. This would help me understand how much emphasis to place on topics in my curriculum during the school year when planning instructional units. Close examination of the format of this sample test tells us that students may be asked to select from four multiple-choice responses, prepare a short written response, directly interpret charts or graphs of data, or interpret political cartoons and the ramifications of what is shown in the cartoon. Students may also be asked to describe problems, issues, or concerns of a specific time period or era based on reading authentic diary entries or letters written by someone from the era or time frame. So that students are comfortable responding to these tasks, teachers should frequently use charts, data tables, political cartoons, and authentic documents in their teaching.

Social Studies Learning and Student Achievement

Helping students understand the vast array of topics under the social studies umbrella can be a daunting task. Knowing the scope of state standards and assessments can help you ensure that your students are prepared in the appropriate content and ready to demonstrate their knowledge as may be required now or in the future. To create deep thinkers who can see connections and analyze situations, it is necessary for students to be involved in hands-on, creative activities that bring the topic to life. This chapter has provided a few suggestions to help you build more analytical thinkers who are able to reflect on our history, our world today, and their role as contributing citizens in the world of tomorrow.

6 | Math

To do well on state math assessments, students must be able to go beyond mere rote and simple computation. They must not only understand the terms and concepts in the mathematical world but also be able to apply those concepts to real-world problems at the application, analysis, and synthesis levels. We see many students today who, although they can manipulate simple algorithms in math class, are at a loss when it comes to actually knowing which mathematical processes to apply to real-life problems. There is often a disconnect between mathematical knowledge and understanding and how math applies to real-world situations. Many students can correctly complete mechanical calculations on a page of workbook problems, but they cannot transfer this information to real-life tasks such as making change, balancing a checkbook, or calculating a percentage reduction on a sale item in a store. This gap between being able to process an algorithm and actually understanding how to apply the mathematical concepts that underlie the process also explains why students in the United States often fail Algebra I when they enter high school: they do not have the deep foundational understandings necessary to apply mathematics appropriately.

According to Deborah Ball (2006), senior researcher for the National Center for Research on Teacher Education, teachers bring into their classrooms their own conceptual understandings about math as well as their ideas and personal feelings about the topic. These influences color how they teach math to their own students. She states that there are several skills teachers need to effectively teach math to their students. She writes:

> Tacit knowledge, whatever its role in independent mathematical activity, is inadequate for teaching. In order to help someone else understand and do mathematics, being able to "do it" oneself is not sufficient. A necessary level of knowledge for teaching involves being able to talk about mathematics, not just describing the steps for following an algorithm, but also about the judgments made and the meanings and reasons for certain relationships or procedures. Explicit knowledge of mathematics entails more than saying the words of mathematical statements or formulas; rather, it must include language that goes beyond the surface representation. Explicit knowledge involves reasons and relationships: being able to explain why, as well as being able to relate particular ideas or procedures to others within mathematics. This is more than "metacognitive awareness" of the processes used in solving a mathematics problem or carrying out a procedure; it includes the ability to talk about and model concepts and procedures. (2006, p. 16)

While many students can select the right multiple-choice response for a simple math test question, they struggle greatly when they have to sort out mathematical information, determine the proper set(s) of algorithms to apply to the situation, and calculate a solution to the given problem without the advantage of predetermined equations or procedures. This chapter will provide many suggestions to help your students begin to go beyond the simple algorithm level so that they can truly understand mathematical concepts and apply the proper procedures to analyze and solve real-world problems.

Instruction's Tie to Performance

As we look at U.S. students' math performance over the years, we find that the problem has not been that state math standards are not rigorous enough; it is more that our instruction has not required students to think deeply enough to understand mathematical concepts at a foundational level. Perhaps we do not have the necessary foundation in math ourselves, we do not understand how to connect math concepts, or we have not created enough activities that help our students transfer their learning to the application level. State standards typically require a much heavier emphasis on hands-on, conceptual instruction than many teachers are currently providing.

Most state standards are organized around the five major concept strands as delineated by the National Council of Teachers of Mathematics (NCTM):

1. Number Sense and Operations
2. Algebra
3. Geometry
4. Measurement
5. Data Analysis and Probability

Within these five broad categories, math concepts and skills have been further delineated into process strands of (1) Procedural Knowledge, (2) Conceptual Understanding, (3) Problem Solving, (4) Reasoning, and (5) Communicating. Clearly, the expectations are that students will be instructed in ways that build procedural knowledge as well as conceptual understanding. Students are also expected to be familiar with problem-solving approaches that emphasize reasoning and communicating thinking.

For many teachers, the math strands contain content that has not been part of the elementary curriculum, such as using logic skills and using writing to explain math thinking, to name but two new concepts. Because much of the content that teachers are now expected to provide to students is higher order and complex, it is essential that any teacher of math clearly understand the concepts and skills of each strand and what students are expected to be able to do at assessment time. The NCTM offers some excellent resources at its Web site to help teachers thoroughly understand the standards expected for each grade level: http://standards.nctm.org/document/eexamples/index.htm.

Many high-quality lesson plans, open-ended activity designs, and evaluation instruments are available on the Web. Some state department Web sites also contain excellent repositories of fully developed lesson plans and actual assessment instruments that teachers can download and use with students. Examples of states that provide teachers with some high-quality resources are Washington, Colorado, and Maryland. Two additional excellent resources for information are the California Score program Web site and the Successlink.org Web site, to name just a few. All of the information for these Web sites, as well as links to other sites of interest in each individual state, can be found in Appendix A.

Appendix A also has resources to help you locate the sample released items for your state as well as any other resources from your state or school district that show how students will be tested. As you read through the sample documents, note which skills and performance levels students will need to demonstrate. Once you have linked state standards to the expected outcomes that your students are likely to encounter on state assessments, you will be much better prepared to help your students meet those expectations at assessment time.

The standards and the released test items will also be helpful for lesson planning. For example, let's pretend that we are responsible for teaching 3rd grade math in the state of New York. The 3rd grade math standards for the state of New York can be found at the New York Department of Education Web site, www.emsc.nysed.gov/3-8/. The list is extensive and detailed and provides guidance to teachers on the expectations for 3rd grade math students. Since this content is very detailed and comprehensive, we can then explore the released items from actual state 3rd grade math assessments to see which skills might be likely to appear on state assessments. This sample document can be found at www.nysedregents.org/testing/mathei/06exams/home.htm. As we view the document, we can jot down the topics and skills covered on the sample assessment. While this list is not all-inclusive and should certainly not limit instruction, it is nonetheless helpful to guide what students will more than likely have to demonstrate on state math assessments at this grade level. Here is the summary of the content contained on this sample assessment:

- Three-column addition with carry
- Sequencing numbers and continuation of patterns
- Standard measure with a ruler
- Place value to hundredths
- Money using coins and bills

- Greater than and less than
- Linking written numbers to numerical representations
- Creating and solving equations from word problems
- Even and odd numbers
- Missing factors
- Using picture arrays for multiplication
- Estimating solutions
- Fractions—linking numerical representations to picture representations
- Telling time
- Identifying geometric forms such as cone, cube, cylinder, and sphere
- Reading and interpreting graphs

If your state provides several years of sample tests for your perusal, you can also review them and add to the concept list any additional concepts that are likely to be tested for your students. When planning instruction, be sure that students have solid skills and understandings for these items. Whatever time is left over can then be devoted to providing foundational skills and concepts that may also be on the list of state standards.

Taking time to analyze released test items to look for commonalities and expectations will go a long way toward helping you understand what your state expects students to know and be able to do at assessment time for your grade level. By asking students to do original thinking rather than simply repeat back equations that have no connection to meaningful work, you will be helping them develop the thinking skills required for success on both short-answer and extended constructed-response test items.

Cognitive Levels of Questions on State Math Assessments

Taking a close look at math assessments around the United States, we see that four cognitive levels of questions might be given to students on state math assessments. The first cognitive level is general mathematical knowledge and skills. Questions in this category might ask students to define terms, identify a mathematical concept, or process basic calculations in symbolic form. They also ask students to use one or more facts, definitions, formulas, or procedures to solve a problem presented in purely mathematical terms. Here are some examples in this category:

- "What is a prime number?"
- "Which of these mathematical sentences shows the distributive property?"
- "$6 + 4 = ?$"
- "$3x + 6 = 27$. Solve for x."
- "Find the value of $(8-2)^2 + 16 \div 4$."

In most cases, the student simply identifies the term or concept or performs the calculation as requested.

The second cognitive level that we might see on state tests is direct application. Questions to test this level of mathematical thinking use one or more facts, definitions, formulas, or procedures to solve a straightforward problem based on real-world situations. The student must consider the situation, identify pertinent information, and determine what mathematical operations are necessary to solve the questions being posed. Examples of questions that require the direct application of mathematical understanding are the following:

Elementary: "Mary's mother brought a plate of 15 cookies to the playground. When she offered the cookies to the children, Mary took 3 cookies, Peter took 4 cookies, and Sam took 6 cookies. How many cookies were still left on the plate?"

Secondary: "Bill wants to buy enough 12 × 12 inch tiles to cover a floor 10 feet wide by 16 feet long. Each box of tile contains 25 tiles and costs $64.00. How many boxes of tile will Bill need to buy, and how much will the tile cost if sales tax is 8 percent of the purchase price?"

The next cognitive level is the "understanding concepts" level. Some state assessments call these questions "brief-answer" or "short" constructed-response items. At this level, questions are framed such that students demonstrate reasoning beyond the literal. Students must process the mathematical concepts, identify concepts and algorithms that are appropriate, derive unstated information, and apply it correctly to the situation. They reach solutions by making inferences or by drawing conclusions from the information provided. Examples of questions in this category are the following:

Elementary: "I have exactly six coins in my pocket whose total value is $1.00. If three of the coins are quarters, what are the other coins in my pocket?"

Secondary: "Bruce is riding in a city cross-country bike marathon. Two-thirds of the course goes uphill. When Bruce rides uphill he can only ride at an average speed of 10 miles per hour. When Bruce is riding downhill, however, he rides at an average speed of 22 miles per hour. What is Bruce's average speed for the whole marathon?"

The final cognitive level of understanding requires students to integrate their conceptual understandings of mathematics to organize information and solve a problem. Students use information as the foundation for thinking about the task and then select their own methods and processes to complete the task. These types of questions frequently form the basis of "extended" constructed-response types of questions. At this level of thinking, students must integrate their understandings of two or more major concepts and organize the information to solve a nonroutine, complex problem. They must also select the appropriate mathematical manipulations needed to suit the situation and often describe the steps they used to process the solution. Here are some examples of these types of questions:

Elementary: "The Ryan family is going to the Ocean Museum from 9 a.m. until 2 p.m. While they are there, they want to see each of the animal and water shows and have time to look at the ocean displays. They will need at least one hour to see the displays. Since they will be at the museum during lunch, they will also need 30 minutes to eat lunch in the museum cafeteria. Use the schedule of event times provided to plan a workable schedule that will allow them to eat lunch, see the displays, and take in each show during their time at the museum."

Secondary: "The City Council is considering opening a new dump, but first it must determine how much longer the existing dump can be used. Using the information provided in the charts about the typical weekly loads currently being brought to the dump and the available space still remaining for waste disposal, calculate how many more weeks of capacity remain before the city will need to open the new facility."

Open-Ended Questions

Study the constructed-response items on your state's sample released items to determine whether students are likely to be given closed- or open-ended constructed-response prompts. Because open-ended questions usually pose the most difficulty for students, we will take a closer look at them here. In addition, constructed-response questions written at the "understanding concepts" or the "integrating concepts" level are often open-ended, which allows students multiple avenues or paths to arrive at solutions that meet the needs of the basic problem.

An example of an open-ended elementary question is "Based on the map, identify five routes that Harry can use to drive from his work to his home." Again, while this example is still not highly complex, there might be 8–10 "acceptable" paths that the student might identify that would be evaluated as "accurate" answers and as an acceptable solution that meets the question's objective. By examining how students respond to an open-response item, you can learn a lot about what they understand and where they still might have questions or even misunderstandings. This insight can save you considerable time as you catch misunderstandings early, before errors are entrenched in a student's thinking.

Another example of an open-response problem might be "Construct eight correct calculations that have an answer equal to 50." In this case, an infinite number of calculations are possible that would all have 50 as the answer. Different students might take very different approaches to meeting the requirements of the prompt.

Open-ended activities can be simple or very complex, requiring students to explore many different ideas and ways to solve the problem. Students learn to monitor and assess their own thinking when teachers value the process of arriving at a solution over getting a "correct" answer. With open-ended problems, the process of selecting and applying the appropriate concepts and skills along the way is most important.

Open-ended activities allow students the freedom to discover new applications for the math concepts so they can go deeper with their thinking and get past the superficial manipulation that has been ineffective in building complex processing skills. Classrooms that highlight open-ended and problem-based activities enjoy dynamic interaction among students as they test their theories and try out their ideas with one another. Students see themselves as "posers" of questions and not just "answerers" of questions. These types of activities provide the most support to helping students become independent, deep thinkers who can really use their mathematical skills for more than just pencil-and-paper drills.

Building Environments That Support High Mathematical Performance

In some states, the area of math performance, and particularly performance on the constructed-response section of the state math assessment, is where the greatest gap exists between high-performing students and low-performing students. Many of the questions that students will face on state math exams require them to use data and algorithms to analyze a problem and actually produce a response, either wholly or at least partially from their own understanding of the underlying math concepts. Therefore, we must help students deepen their level of understanding and their ability to function in this area. Using high-quality assessments in the math classroom can help you identify developmentally appropriate content for your students, recognize student misconceptions, and determine whether your instruction is effective in altering those misconceptions.

Brain Power

One of the reasons that student learning in math has often been superficial has to do with how the brain learns. Each of us has two types of memory systems, the declarative (or explicit) memory system and the procedural (or implicit) memory system. Procedural memories are those things that we know how to do but often are difficult to verbalize. Examples in this category are riding a bicycle, being able to type or to swim, or even driving to work without consciously thinking about the path to get to work. Procedural memories are those things that we can do on "autopilot" because they are so well ingrained in our memories. Procedural memory is very durable and long-term.

The declarative memory system is made up of semantic memory and episodic memory. *Semantic memory* refers to factual knowledge that we have deliberately learned without reference to a time or place context. Semantic memories are facts and understandings such as the names of the state capitals, the times tables, or various math formulas. After continued practice, we can "parrot" these things from memory without much deliberate thought. People who have good semantic memories are good at trivia games and can often provide much information on topics of interest to them.

Episodic memory encompasses memories tied to a specific time and place. These memories often are associated with emotions, and they deepen with the strength of the emotion attached to them. These are the types of memories we carry when events have had a significant impact on us, such as a car accident or a wedding. When we recall episodic memories, the event is almost as real in our minds as it was when it originally occurred, and we can recall many of the emotions we experienced during the event. While semantic memory stores information that we deliberately try to remember, episodic memories are stored regardless of our interest or intent in remembering these things.

Memory, Manipulatives, and Hands-On Learning

When students use manipulatives or are engaged in project-based math activities, the information gets stored in both the semantic and episodic memory banks. When memories are so stored, learning is more effective, more meaningful, and more deeply rooted in our brains.

Most math teachers have probably received some training in using manipulatives and hands-on activities with students; however, they may not have completely understood why combining hands-on learning with math concepts is a beneficial idea for deep learning. If you think back to some of the most effective lessons you have experienced, you will probably remember that this lesson also had some links to things or hands-on components. Perhaps you conducted interviews with someone or built something or researched something in great detail. You probably did not work by yourself on this project but more than likely worked with or at least interacted with others at least some of the time during the activity. You probably also have some pleasant memories associated with this activity, such as receiving an award or nice praise.

When I have talked to teachers about the connection between hands-on learning and math retention, two objections always seem to surface. The first objection boils down to the fact that some teachers are unsure about how to use these activities effectively. Some teachers feel that manipulatives or hands-on activities, though fun for students, do not always seem to help students understand math concepts more deeply, so they are reluctant to use them regularly. Others find the higher energy level and verbal interaction that usually accompany such lessons uncomfortable. So, again, they are reluctant to use such activities. Because they aren't certain about how to best use these activities, they see changes in classroom management as an unwelcome challenge. The second objection that teachers often make about hands-on learning is that it takes too long to teach in this manner. Although they may try an open-ended or hands-on activity here and there, they quickly revert back to more skill-drill types of activities because they feel the pressure to cover more curriculum content.

Let's address these objections by examining the use of manipulatives in the math classroom. Manipulatives are good for introducing students to a new concept and helping them understand how things work at the most basic level. Although students do find using manipulatives fun and interesting, our objective in using them is to help students see at a very concrete level just how the math concept works. After students can observe the concept at work, the manipulatives are no longer needed or effective for deepening understanding. The mistake that many teachers make is that after introducing the concept with manipulatives, we do not go on to create linking lessons that transition students back to the shorthand we used to stand for these concepts—

the math symbols and equations. Students have sometimes failed to make the connection between what they observed at the hands-on level and the abstract symbols because teachers failed to use bridge activities that helped students connect what they learned at the episodic level with what they learned at the semantic level.

Here is an example of a bridge activity to link the manipulative lesson to the symbolic mathematical form. To introduce the concept of adding negative and positive integers to students, my students and I created a number line by laying down masking tape on the classroom floor and marking numbers in both positive and negative directions from zero. Students quickly learned to add and subtract using the number line by walking out the proper steps to see how negatives and positives affected their movement on the number line. Once students understood the concept, we then went back to examining this issue using simply the mathematical symbols for this operation. When students became confused, they were reminded to visualize the floor's number line and how they had physically walked out the same operation. What might have taken a couple of weeks to learn working at only the semantic side was greatly condensed to only a couple of days by adding an episodic element. Needless to say, in the future, when faced with operations involving positive and negative numbers, these students have an episodic memory that will always enhance and reinforce their recall of how to perform the semantic operation.

This brings me to the second criticism—that teaching in hands-on ways takes too much time. As can be seen from the performance of the students with negative and positive numbers, when students truly understand the underlying concepts behind what they are learning, it actually shortens learning time while also deepening the connections the brain makes around this information. For my "number line" students, learning was permanent and deep. When teachers feel pressured to cover the curriculum, superficial learning occurs that does not transfer to the higher levels of thinking. When you design your lessons, think about how you can connect semantic knowledge with episodic (hands-on) information. Learning that is truly effective is "a mile deep and an inch wide," not the other way around.

Learning Concepts from the Five Math Strands

While examining the state math standards and sample assessments in detail is the surest way to improve student performance on state math assessments, we can also use some other strategies to encourage students to think deeply about math concepts and practice the appropriate thinking patterns. Let's examine the strands one by one to establish each one's key learning concepts.

For the first strand, Number Sense and Operations, young children should practice counting and skip-counting activities accompanied by rhythmic actions such as clapping or snapping to help establish this foundational knowledge in semantic memory. For older children, this is the strand where math raps and math fact repetition become important again for background semantic knowledge. As students advance into middle and high school, reinforcement in the number sense area helps students learn how to manipulate numeric symbols and realize numbers are simply symbols that can be used in many ways to represent the same concept.

This first strand is also about building mental math skills, building estimation skills, organizing data, using formulas and algorithms, and learning terminology and proper math vocabulary. We should remind students to use appropriate terminology and to interpret and compare numbers in many ways. We should also ask them to explain their mathematical processes and thinking and to explain their calculations using words, numbers, and symbols as appropriate. Rather than simply asking for answers, you should probe student ideas and thinking. Monitor students' conceptual understandings more than whether the answer is right or wrong. Ask students to "explain their thinking" or "justify their answer" or to "think through" orally their steps and approaches rather than simply allowing them to wait for you to guide them through their mathematical calculations.

Preparation in the second strand, Algebra, is about looking at patterns, relationships, and functions. Algebra involves representing math structures and models in symbolic form and examining qualitative relationships. Even young elementary students should learn about patterns and relationships. Algebra allows us to analyze relationships and change in various contexts. Older elementary students should learn about completing patterns, analyzing numeric relationships, and analyzing function relationships by using "missing numbers," "function machine," or "What's my rule?" activities. Middle and high school students continue to advance their understandings about comparing numeric relationships and representing them in symbolic form. They must learn to take real-world problems and convert them into symbolic form—for example, by writing equations to solve story problems or real-life problems.

Geometry, the third strand, covers geometric concepts and the properties of shape and spatial relationships. Students must learn about the properties of one- to three-dimensional shapes, develop an understanding about spatial relationships and reasoning, be able to visualize geometric problems and dimensional shapes, and also understand the concepts of symmetry. Young students should be able to identify shapes and the dimensions of shape. They should also be able to examine relationships between those shapes, while older elementary students should begin to learn about the spatial relationships of shapes and symmetry. Middle and high school students should begin to visualize these relationships and be able to apply the concepts they have learned about size and shape to real-world problems.

In the fourth strand, Measurement, students should explore standard and nonstandard ways to measure and use the tools of measurement; identify attributes; move between metric and standard units of measure; and work with formulas such as those for scale, ratio, proportion, velocity, and density on an age-appropriate basis. For young students, this involves identifying shapes and attributes and learning to use the tools of measurement. Older students should be learning to function within the measurement systems, identify attributes, and apply the appropriate formulas and algorithms for finding solutions to real-world problems.

Strand 5, Data Analysis and Probability, requires students to formulate questions and to collect and analyze data to answer those questions. In this strand, students are expected not only to create the question but also to prepare appropriate displays of the data that lead to interpretations based on the patterns and inferences seen in the organized data. Not only do students develop and evaluate inferences around data, but they also make predictions about future events and probability factors. Young students can gather data, study patterns, and learn to represent data graphically. Older elementary students can begin to make inferences from graphs and charts and to make predictions about future events based on the analysis of the data. Middle and high school students should be able to gather original data, organize the data, make predictions, and calculate probabilities of various occurrences based on their data analysis.

Constructed-Response Questions for the Math Strands

Let's examine a couple of typical constructed-response questions closely to see what skills students would need to successfully answer them. The first question is from the Geometry strand; it is similar to a released item found at a state Web site for 8th grade constructed-response items:

Three new schools have been built in one section of a growing city. The local Parks Department would like to locate a park equidistant from the three schools so that all of the students from each of the three schools can use the park.

Using the diagram and geometric construction, determine where the new park should be built. Explain the steps that you used to solve the problem using words and symbols as needed to explain your thinking. Provide evidence that the location you have indicated is equidistant from all three schools.

To create a correct and complete answer that would justify receiving all possible points, students must first read and understand the task. Second, they must be able to use the appropriate tools and apply the right geometrical operation to find the point equidistant from the three given points. Once students have done this, they then must not only explain their thinking but also organize a meaningful explanation of their process, including evidence that the point chosen meets the criteria of being equidistant from all three schools. Put more simply—and from our point of view as math teachers—we will need to teach, monitor, and reinforce the following skills throughout the school year:

• Ensure that students know how to use any geometric tools such as a compass, ruler, or protractor by asking them to demonstrate their use on a regular basis.

• Ensure that students can choose and apply the correct mathematical process to solve geometric problems they might encounter on the state assessment.

• Require students to write explanations about how they solved problems in an organized and clear manner.

• Require students to cite evidence that demonstrates appropriate solutions.

Let's examine another extended constructed-response activity—this one from the Algebra math strand—to see again what might be required of a student to perform well on that question:

A toy maker builds dollhouses and wagons. It costs $20 each to build a dollhouse and $30 each to build a wagon. The amount available to produce all dollhouses and wagons in one week is $1,200. Let d represent each dollhouse built and w represent each wagon built. The equation for the cost of making the toys for one week is $20d + 30w = 1,200$.

1. On the grid provided, construct a graph of this equation using correct labels and scales.

2. The toy maker sells two wagons for every dollhouse he sells. Write an equation that shows the number of wagons sold in relation to the number of dollhouses sold. Show this second equation on the graph also with correct labels and scales.

3. Calculate how many dollhouses and wagons the toy maker can build per week based on the cost to build each toy and the amount of money available to build complete toys each week.

4. Explain how the graph can help you prove your answer.

In this case, students must understand the concept of equations and variables. They must understand how to plot an equation on a graph, solve the equations (discarding fractional toy components) in the problem, and explain how the graph proves that the answer is correct. Again, just as in the first example, this question has clear implications for ongoing math instruction that can help students become more comfortable with questions that require this level of complexity.

Since most states also ask students to respond to multiple-choice math questions, a simple and fun way to keep students sharp in this area is by periodically playing "quiz" games like Jeopardy! or Brain Quest every couple of weeks with your students for an hour or so. You can also keep index card "decks" of these questions available for filling in on those "extra class minutes" that pop up now and again. Again, by going through the standards and the released assessments, you can develop a wealth of material for such quick and interesting games. As we discussed, routine repetition and practice deepen and reinforce semantic memory information.

Helping Students Learn to Self-Evaluate

According to an old adage, "We learn best from our own mistakes." This is certainly true in the math classroom. When we ask students to monitor, evaluate, and improve their own work, they develop a much deeper level of understanding. Getting the "right answer" is only one small part of learning and "doing" math. The rest is about the thinking process and how the student processes the task. In far too many classrooms, the emphasis has been on getting the "right" answer rather than on the thinking the student used to solve the problem.

We can help our students by exposing them frequently to open-ended, higher-order tasks that require them to slingshot their thinking off one another. We can teach them to use rubrics to evaluate the work of the group as well as their own individual work. When students are able to understand what causes one response to be scored a 2 while another response merits a 4, it becomes more clear to them how they must refine their own work.

The example in Figure 6.1 provides some ideas for how you can construct rubrics for use in the math class. For younger students, be sure to write your rubric in words that your students can clearly understand. A quick search on the Internet for math rubrics can also provide many outstanding examples and design tools that you can use to quickly create rubrics. One such free resource that is easy to use is the rubric creator available at http://rubistar.4teachers.org. Additional information on rubrics can be found in Appendix B.

Be sure to also examine any math rubrics that your state uses to score student work. Again, if necessary, translate these documents into language appropriate for the age level with which you work. Occasionally allow students time to identify ways to improve their work. This helps them get used to thinking through problems more carefully and making needed revisions.

Writing in the Math Class

Being able to communicate one's ideas and the logical procedures that have been followed in a clear, deliberate, sequential manner is a vital skill that students will need for success in their lives. When we write, we must gather, organize, and clarify our thinking so that others can understand our ideas, methods, and strategies. Writing about mathematical thinking can help students understand and clarify their own thoughts and ideas, and it can also provide teachers with a window into what the student understands or misunderstands.

Asking students to write about their strategies, their thinking, and their justifications makes sense and will help students move beyond superficial thinking about the work they do in math class. Indeed, the NCTM lists communication as a goal for student math performance. Its standards (available at http://standards.nctm.org/document/chapter7/comm.htm) specify that all students should be able to do the following tasks:

FIGURE 6.1
Sample Math Student Rubric

Student Rubric

4 Points: Student response shows complete understanding of all parts of the problem. Student chooses a logical and reasonable strategy that leads to a correct solution to the problem with no mathematical errors. Student provides supportive information such as drawings, graphs, or numbers as appropriate. Student provides a clear explanation or justification for the processes used. Student demonstrates solid evidence of analyzing the situation in mathematical terms and thinking through all aspects of the problem during completion of the task.

3 Points: Student response shows general comprehension of the problem. Student chooses a logical and reasonable solution, but the mathematics or strategy may have minor errors that do not impede the overall solution. Despite the problems, the solution may be correct or fairly close to being correct. Student provides some drawings, graphs, or numbers but may leave out some support items that would have provided more clarity. Student's explanation may be feasible but not fully developed or somewhat incomplete. Student demonstrates some evidence of analyzing the problem in mathematical terms and thinking through a solution.

2 Points: Student response shows mixed evidence of understanding of the problem. Some steps may be correct, but the work is incomplete or shows gaps in understanding of the concepts or mathematical skills needed to solve the problem. Student makes an attempt but is unable to develop a correct solution to the problem. Student may not include graphs, drawings, or numbers that might have clarified the solution to the problem. Student demonstrates little evidence of being able to analyze the problem in mathematical terms or developing a solution.

1 Point: Student shows minimal understanding of the problem. Most of the work is incorrect and does not lead to a meaningful solution to the problem. Student makes either a minimal attempt to solve the problem or no attempt. Student provides no graphs, drawings, or numbers to document ideas or strategies and is unable to develop a reasonable solution to the problem.

My Self-Assessment _____

My Group's Assessment _____

Teacher's Assessment _____

• Organize and consolidate their mathematical thinking through communication.

• Communicate their mathematical thinking coherently and clearly to peers, teachers, and others.

• Analyze and evaluate the mathematical thinking and strategies of others.

• Use the language of mathematics to express mathematical ideas precisely.

Many states are moving to include more short or extended constructed-response questions on their state assessments as they revamp their current test instruments. The large majority of these questions require that students "justify" or "explain" their thinking in words, pictures, and symbols. Because writing helps students think sequentially about ideas and the steps they have taken, writing needs to become an important part of the math classroom. For example, when students are working, ask them to write about their thinking processes and the strategies they are attempting to use even if they are unclear about the appropriate methodology needed to solve the problem. Not only might it help you see where their understandings are unclear or their thinking may be going awry, but it may also help them think through and verbalize what it is that is confusing for them. This is a good habit to develop, because even if they do not get full credit for solving a problem on a state exam's constructed-response item, by writing at least something for the item, they may manage to receive some points even if they cannot complete their answer fully and correctly.

Math Instruction That Supports Deep Thinking

To think deeply in math, students need to be able to examine a problem, state it clearly in their minds, and then know how to systematically ask the questions that will help them solve the problem. They must formulate theories, gather data, refine their thinking, and verify their theories with sound logic and sensible mathematical analysis. Students must summarize what information they know and be able to pinpoint what information they still need to appropriately analyze the data. Furthermore, they must be able to communicate their thinking and provide evidence to demonstrate that their thinking makes sense and can lead to an acceptable solution.

One of my favorite Web sites for fun activities for teaching math at all levels is www.coollessons.org/coolunits.htm. At this site, you will find links to a large collection of ideas and ready-made, hands-on lesson plans, Weblinks for Webquests, and information on helping students do online research, as well as other project-based teaching ideas. In addition to the Web resources found in Appendix B, some other excellent Web sites specifically for fun math activities for both teachers and students are http://cte.jhu.edu/techacademy/web/2000/heal/mathsites.htm, www.mathsisfun.com/, and http://web.media.mit.edu/~reilly/mmis-mar-apr04.html.

Too often in American math classes we have asked students to solve the "simple" when what has really been needed has been practice solving the complex and "messy" work that typifies the kind of problems found in real-life mathematics. We have asked students to reproduce and repeat rather than to think deeply and create their own work and their own solutions. This has resulted in shallow learning, with little transfer to the application level. If we want students who can really use mathematics and think in mathematical terms, we must let our students practice with these "messy" ideas and concepts. If this is to happen, our role must become one of guiding and directing the investigation process and asking the questions that will lead students to reaffirm or reassess their mathematical approach as needed. In short, our role must be to assist with and clarify the learning process—not do the thinking for the student. When we approach math instruction from this perspective, we will be creating students who can truly function in the mathematical realm.

7 | Building and Supporting Student Achievement

How Can Assessments Help Me Improve Instruction?

If we are to help our students become independent and deep thinkers, we must change our view of our role in the process. We must abandon the view of a teacher as the keeper and dispenser of knowledge and move to a model where teaching means observing and diagnosing students' current level of performance and then providing guidance that can help them advance their skills and understandings to the next level. While there is no question that knowledge is important, what makes the difference is the ability to locate the appropriate information and then process and apply that information at the right time and in the right way. Many state standards require higher-level thinking and reasoning skills. If we are to help students acquire learning for life, rather than just pass a test, we must raise the performance bar beyond mere memorization.

One of the reasons that many teachers balk at what they term "teaching to the test" is because they cannot see past the "individual" or minute skills that they believe state assessments require of students. They have difficulty connecting the seemingly disjointed questions to the broader curriculum and the standards they have been asked to teach. Although the tests may seem isolated and unrelated to the overarching goals of instruction in the classroom, nothing could be further from the truth. The skills that students need to perform well on constructed-response or problem-based assessments are actually much more complex than what might be first perceived. Because state-released items are meant to provide teachers with a guide of what the actual state test will be like, we can examine a sample question to test this idea.

Let's consider the issue of complexity by looking at a sample assessment question from the released items on the Department of Education Web site for the 8th grade language arts test from Massachusetts. On the selected sample item, students are asked to read a three-paragraph excerpt from "A Walk to the Jetty" from *Annie John* by Jamaica Kincaid. Students then have seven multiple-choice questions and one constructed-response item based on this short passage. Using this one text passage, let's see what understandings and skills students need to respond to this question.

When we categorize the seven multiple-choice questions, we see that one question directly asks for an interpretation of how a word is used in the passage, one asks students to identify the part of speech of a word in a sentence, one asks students to determine the author's word choice in a specific sentence, one requires literal recall of information directly stated in the passage, and the remaining three questions ask students to chose a response by making an inference. Clearly, the expectation is that students will demonstrate higher-order thinking, because six of the seven questions require higher-order processing skills to some degree.

If I am an 8th grade language arts teacher hoping to prepare my students for success on this assessment, it is clear that my students must be well prepared to draw inferences from text, analyze and discuss the author's word choice, and demonstrate the ability to interpret vocabulary meaning from context. We can learn all this from analyzing just one sample question.

Continuing our analysis of this sample item, we then find a constructed-response question addressing this same text passage: "Identify and explain the mixed feelings the speaker has about leaving her home. Use relevant and specific information from the excerpt to support your answer." Again, not only must students be able to identify passage tone, but they must also be able to "interpret" and draw conclusions about the writer's attitudes and emotions from the text. Once students have identified these important concepts, they must then "cite evidence" to support their conclusions as well as construct a meaningful, well-organized essay to convey their ideas. Classroom instruction must help students learn to interpret a writer's viewpoint and draw a conclusion, compose a quality essay, and link meaningful passages to provide support for ideas and conclusions. Again, these are complex concepts for most 8th grade students.

Teachers as Coaches

Learning is an active process, but it has been treated as a passive activity in far too many classrooms. If we view ourselves as guides and coaches, how we behave in the classroom significantly changes. Let's consider how a coach might approach teaching to see what differences there might be.

If I were a golf coach, I would not give my students a pencil-and-paper test to identify what they know and can do. Instead, I would place them on a golf course and ask them to *show* me what they can do by asking them to swing a golf club at an actual golf ball. As I watched the students perform the task, I would note such subskills as timing, form, pacing, body alignment, proficiency in selecting and applying the right club for the situation, and so forth. I would make notes as I watched and quickly identify the skill level of each student in each subskill or standard. Some students obviously would demonstrate strong abilities, whereas some students might not be able to hit the ball at all. As the coach, my job is to determine which skills seem to be strong as well as which ones seem to need further refinement and then plan appropriate activities to move students to the next levels. This information on performance would help me guide students to continue practicing the things they do well so that they are motivated and comfortable continuing the activity, but it also reminds me to present activities that can slowly build and shape those skills that need refinement and development. Armed with good assessment information, I would group my students by skill area and plan activities that would help them feel confident and enjoy the game and, at the same time, result in more proficient skills and greater overall performance.

Over time, as a result of building on strengths, students would become more capable and more confident. Some may catch on quickly and advance to new groups, while some may need to spend more time continuing to practice just hitting the ball. Helping students understand what "good" looks like will enable them to self-analyze and self-correct as they learn. Patient support along with guided and focused instruction will build student skill and confidence on the way to high performance.

Although some teachers do function exactly as the coach in this example and truly do a great job of customizing learning to meet individual needs, that is not always the case in classrooms across the United States. Some teachers have tried to use a "one size fits all" or "teaching to the middle" instructional approach for all students. Others have focused the majority of their instruction time and attention on the students of only one subgroup of the class. Often this might be the lowest-performing students because the performance gaps are the greatest and thus the most evident. Neither approach will produce the kind of high performance and student success that we are seeking. If we go back to our golf analogy, this would be like having the whole class continue to practice how to properly hold and swing the golf club irrespective of the fact that a young "Michelle Wie" and a few others in the class were already competent players ready to work on improving their timing or drive length.

If we are to help our students reach their potential, we must identify what students do well and organize our class to meet the differences in skill and ability. Although the standards of superior performance remain the same, we must customize instruction so that groups of students can work together on their own needs to improve their overall performance on the task. If many students fail to demonstrate mastery, we must reexamine our instructional delivery to see what went wrong. If only a few students scored poorly on a given skill, group and reteach these students without slowing down the rest of the students who are ready to move on to more complex tasks. Just as the golf coach continues to watch and assess performance to determine next steps, so too must we organize our classes so that ongoing diagnosis can drive instruction.

Another concept about state test construction that we must understand is that although each discipline has a set of standards that identify what to teach in each content area, not all standards are created equal. If we analyze how state tests have been developed for each grade level, we will see that some standards are assessed quite heavily, whereas others may be only briefly assessed or even omitted altogether. This knowledge helps us identify which things we must ensure that students have mastered and which things, although introduced and practiced, are not a priority for our time and attention.

As mentioned throughout this book, some states provide background information on test construction or "blueprints" for state testing to help teachers understand their state's priorities. These documents map which standards are considered nonnegotiable and identify how much of the assessment is devoted to each skill or concept. If your state has such a document, it is essential that you study this information to clearly understand what skills are likely to appear on assessments. Some skills are only briefly tested or even omitted altogether, so less instructional time can be spent in these areas. Once you have identified which skills are heavily, moderately, and only slightly tested, you can match this information with your knowledge of where each student is on the continuum of mastery. Which students are "just learning the game," and which ones are ready for skill refinement or advanced work?

Designing Activities That Deepen Thinking and Performance

Once you have identified what skills or understandings students will have to demonstrate and how they currently perform, you are ready to design activities that help students demonstrate their level of mastery and at the same time strengthen their own skills. The activities can be simple, such as a short constructed-response activity that students complete in one sitting, or they can consist of more complex performance activities or "authentic" activities that present students with a more challenging problem to solve over several days or periods. While skill development has its place in our teaching "bag of tricks," sometimes we are too quick to break learning down into too many subskills. When we do, we take some of the joy and challenge out of learning for our students.

For example, sometimes students need to take all of the information they have and struggle with coming up with a solution based on combining their thoughts, ideas, and background knowledge. If we expect students to learn at the conceptual level, then we need to provide some activities that challenge them to think and experiment on their own to solve problems. If we want students to demonstrate original thought and creative thinking abilities, then we need to allow them time to explore problems and experiment with solutions until they find solutions that work. As we have all learned through our life experiences, sometimes learning what does *not* work is the best path to learning what does work.

Authentic learning activities that require students to use their accumulated knowledge are perfect for preparing students to think independently and thoroughly. Project-based instruction is a great way to motivate students and get them excited and deeply involved in learning. While some teachers feel that project-based learning takes too much time, it often leads to learning that is more intense and personal—and thus deeper and more complete. If you are not familiar with project-based teaching, a good source of information is the Northwest Regional Education Laboratory (2002).

Here is the sequence for developing either a constructed-response activity or a more complex learning project. First, select the standard that you want students to meet, and then think about the ways students in your state are asked to demonstrate mastery. What should that look like? Think about the types of tasks students will face on their content assessment. In all likelihood, they will be expected to use or respond to a stimulus such as a chart, quote, text passage, map, diagram, problem, or other similar item. Will they be asked to respond to a poem or evaluate a document? Should they be able to analyze or explain a system or cycle? Will they need to derive information from a map or chart or use the information to create a graphic organizer? From the typical response patterns that students might see, select a stimulus. Your activity should require students to do something tangible and concrete so you can easily see how well they perform the given task. Once you have determined the stimulus to be used for the activity, determine what students will be asked to do. Will they be asked to read and evaluate something? Will they be asked to compare or contrast information or viewpoints? Will they be asked to analyze, make a prediction, or summarize something? What are the expectations for performance? As you create your activity, stretch student thinking by moving from the concrete "what" to the more abstract "why."

Linking Instruction with Assessment

Taking language arts as an example, let's think about the ways students are assessed. Since we know that state tests will require students to analyze aspects of text, we might ask them to read a poem and write a couple of paragraphs describing how the author used imagery in the poem. If we know that students are often asked to read a short text excerpt and compare and contrast two characters, we could design activities that ask our students to do exactly that. If we want to extend that process into a longer instructional time frame, we might ask students to read two stories or two novels and then compare and contrast them. The format of the task should mirror the segment that students will be expected to do on the state assessment but in a more complex form. We will use this opportunity to guide and shape instruction as well as to provide feedback on student performance.

Once you have designed a student activity, the next step is to take the assessment yourself or ask a colleague in your area to take the assessment for you and give you feedback. As you respond, try to view the task from your students' perspective. Although responses will vary, try to identify as many possible answers or ways of solving the problem as might be acceptable. What are some of the difficulties your students might have? Can you eliminate these problems by reworking your prompt or task? Taking the test yourself will help you spot potential trouble spots so that you can rework the item to improve it. When we know our students can perform a comparison on a longer, more complex work—as in this example—we also know that they can do the same task on a brief text passage that may appear on the state exam. When our instruction is at the more complex level, state assessments become easy tasks for our students, and they perform well.

Other content areas can also design assessments using this procedure. Consider the recommendations from the appropriate content chapters in this book, and think about what your students will be expected to do on their state assessments. For example, in math, we might ask students to read about an elaborate problem and to create an appropriate set of steps and algorithms to solve the problem, or we might give them a real-life problem to set up and solve on their own. In social studies, we might provide a diary excerpt and ask students to draw conclusions about what life was like during a specific time period, or we might ask them to make predictions about political feelings of a certain era by analyzing a political cartoon. In science, we might provide a set of journal notes and ask students to determine whether an appropriate scientific investigation had been conducted, or we might spend more time asking students to actually set up and conduct their own scientific experiments rather than simply read about scientific theories from a textbook. Whenever possible, try to find real-world, authentic tasks that deal with contemporary issues that add relevance and meaning for students so that they can truly show what they know and are able to do. These are just a small sampling of the types of activities that can mirror what students will be asked to do at assessment time. Many outstanding Web resources, project-based learning ideas, simulations, and lesson plan ideas are also provided in Appendix B. Just like golf students practice various skills that make up the whole of playing golf, students must be comfortable with the process and find responding to similar tasks second nature.

Once we have designed the task, the next part of our work needs to be teaching students how to organize their thinking and respond appropriately to the task. Often teachers skip this very important step and then wonder why their students do not do well on the wonderful task they have designed. Just as the student learning golf must be shown how to apply just the right amount of force to direct the ball where it needs to go, students need to have specific training and deliberate strategies for approaching the tasks they will be asked to perform.

Let's think again about a language arts task we might give to our students. Many language arts assessments ask students to read a text, think about what is being asked in the prompt, and form a response that uses information from the passage as well as their own background knowledge—a quite complex task. Just as the golf ball flew into the water when not properly supported with good training, when we do not provide our students with guidance and direction to do a task, student performance can break down.

We need to help students understand the thinking behind approaching the task. One way to do this is to summarize the appropriate steps for students on a classroom strategy chart. Students can continue to monitor this chart as they are learning to apply the appropriate thinking skills. For example, high school students might be given the following list of suggestions for responding to a short text-based constructed-response prompt:

1. Read the question and determine what you are being asked to do in the prompt. If necessary, write it in your own words.

2. Reread the directions, highlighting all important words or phrases that will help you identify what the prompt is asking you to do.

3. Highlight information from the passage that will help you support your thoughts and ideas. Make notes about key points that you might want to include in your response.

4. Think about how best to organize your answer. Organize your ideas in a graphic organizer if it will help you think more clearly.

5. Extend and clarify your answer by including information from your personal experience, or add information you already know about the topic.

6. Be sure to support your answer by including important quotes from the text with the comma-quote format when appropriate.

7. If possible, conclude with a statement about why this information is important. Use concluding phases such as "This means," or "In other words," or "In summary" to clearly communicate your viewpoint and your understanding of the text.

Now that students have a guideline for developing a response, model how to apply this strategy until students can clearly process responses on their own. Using the think-aloud strategy and sample text, model for students how to go through the instructions in a step-by-step fashion, applying each reminder to developing their response.

Help students understand exactly what "good" looks like in a response. As students develop solid responses, be sure to keep sample papers, referred to as "anchor papers." This will help students see solid examples of what they are expected to do. As students practice generating responses, talk through some effective samples from the class. Point out what the author has done that helps improve the response. This will help students learn to identify what a high-quality response looks like and sounds like. It is hard to understand what high quality is and hone our own skills without a comparison model.

As you are developing constructed-response items to sample student performance and understandings, try to avoid some common pitfalls. For example, be sure that the questions you are asking truly require higher-level thinking rather than just listing information found in a text passage. For some outstanding examples of complex higher-order tasks that both engage students and require higher-level thinking, see the Department of Education for the state of Washington Web site at www.k12.wa.us/assessment. Washington educators have developed several excellent instructional units for all content areas that teachers can use to help students think deeply and show their learning. In addition, several top-notch videos describing how to create assessments and strong instructional lessons are available in the video library section of the George Lucas Educational Foundation Edutopia Web site: www.edutopia.org.

As students practice with activities such as these, you can clearly observe both their capabilities and areas of need. Did the students understand what they were asked to do? Do they have the skills necessary to construct a solid response or perform the requested task? What follow-up or clarification might be necessary? What skills still need to be practiced? Were the expectations for performance met? What support is needed to enhance an already-good response to make it even better? What advanced work can you provide to stimulate additional refinement or new learning for these students? What support is needed by students still struggling with the task? When we address these factors, we can deepen learning and better meet the needs of all students in the diverse classroom.

Training Students to Self-Evaluate

Just as it would be hard to drive a golf ball into the cup while wearing a blindfold, it is difficult for students to hit a target they do not clearly understand. In the past, students have often tried to "guess" what the teacher wanted through experience and trial and error. After participating in class discussions and taking a few teacher-constructed assessments, more successful students are able to anticipate what the teacher has deemed important and what the typical "test" might cover. This approach builds neither student skills nor learning independence.

By providing our students with clear, detailed rubrics written in age-appropriate language, we can not only begin to share with our students what is important but also help them compare their own work to the standard for excellence. If you have not used rubrics much and need some additional information about them, including guidance on how to develop high-quality documents, PAREonline.net is one of the many outstanding Internet resources on this topic. You can find this resource at http://pareonline.net/getvn.asp?v=7&n=25. Some additional sites with great information on rubrics can be found in Appendix B.

Working Together to Raise Student Performance

One of the more positive changes in education during the last few years has been a movement on the part of many educators to create more collaborative school environments, where teachers come together around real questions and problems. These are organizations where teachers have taken steps to reduce isolation by increasing opportunities to share ideas and work together for student success. In these schools, one-shot or "one size fits all" professional development has been minimized or even eliminated in favor of focused, professional learning groups who work together to study instructional practice and student performance.

Schools that have made this philosophical change are becoming more and more common. In these schools, grade-level or subject-based work groups have remolded themselves as supportive team members who plan together, work collaboratively with one another, seek answers to their own questions, and share successful strategies and techniques in their mission to improve student performance. It is truly improvement "from the inside out" rather than "from the outside in" in these schools. Collaborative efforts in organizations such as these have helped teachers feel more confident knowing that they have a solid support system to ensure not only student success but also teacher success. In these successful schools, teachers have made it a priority to discuss and observe one another teach, reflect on successful practice, focus on designing quality lessons to teach troublesome concepts, and collaboratively examine student work. These teams make it a priority to meet regularly, discuss their challenges and successes, and plan together to develop lessons that better present skills and concepts to students. In such a dynamic environment, teams are finding phenomenal success for their efforts.

Coming together around standards and student performance by grade level or by content area is an excellent way to raise a school's overall performance. When the walls of isolation and individualism come down, performance goes up. Joyce and Showers (2002) state:

> During the past few years, research on training has documented the benefits of peers helping peers in the implementation of an innovation. Regular, structured interaction between or among peers over substitutive content is one of the hallmarks of a profession and is viewed by other professionals as essential professional nourishment rather than a threat to autonomy. (p. 82)

As these authors point out, other professionals such as doctors, dentists, lawyers, and even hairdressers rely on the experience and professional opinions of others to help them make better decisions for their clients. For far too long, educators have had little professional interaction with their peers over the day-to-day problems they face, the decisions they make, and the practices they use in their own classrooms. When teachers work to develop a climate that encourages continuous study of effective practice, shared reflection, and unilateral commitment to the improvement of teaching, lasting and meaningful school improvement will take place. Joyce and Showers cite clear research that supports the fact that in schools where the staff take time to ask the hard questions, examine the effectiveness of their own instructional practices, and study the relationship between their actions and student learning, achievement soars.

One of the first collaborative activities that a staff may want to do, either by grade level or by content area, is to jointly examine the standards and the released items for their state so that they can compare notes on what resources and instructional strategies each member of the team might have on ways to build student skills in each area. A natural outcome of these discussions might be that teachers will find new ways to share lesson ideas or strategies, coteach, or observe one another teaching a particular strategy. With more ideas to toss around during lesson planning, outstanding solutions to improving student learning result.

The next step in the process is examining samples of actual student work. Taking time to analyze samples of student work and provide feedback to one another on students' problems or strengths can be an eye-opening and helpful process, especially for less experienced teachers. While it is beyond the scope of this book to delve deeply into the process of examining student work samples, many helpful resources on the Web and in print can help teachers effectively study student work samples (see, e.g., Langer, Colton, & Goff, 2003). Some other helpful books on examining student work are *A Facilitator's Book of Questions: Resources for Looking Together at Student and Teacher Work* by Allen and Blythe (2003); *Looking Together at Student Work* by Blythe, Allen, and Powell (1999); and *Assessing Student Learning: From Grading to Understanding* by D. Allen (1998). You can view a video entitled *Looking at Student Work: A Window into the Classroom* at the Annenberg Institute for School Reform (1997) Website and also read an article about by Graham and Fahey in the March 1999 issue of *Educational Leadership*.

Viewing samples of what students "know and are able to do" can give you a coach's perspective on which concepts or skills students understand and which still need refinement. When teachers truly become collaborative partners, it can build grade or department cohesion, reduce feelings of isolation, foster new ideas, clarify performance expectations, and expand the entire team's effectiveness with students.

Developing assessments that measure the skills and standards that students are expected to master is the next step in the collaborative process. Teachers who teach the same grade level or content area can also work together to develop not only better lesson content but also carefully crafted constructed-response assessments and rubric guides that the whole team can share. A natural outcome of such teamwork will undoubtedly be rich discussions as to curriculum content. In addition, the team members will help each other establish and clarify student performance expectations as they work together to identify anchor papers and exemplars that meet the criteria for each scoring level. This step is especially helpful for new or less experienced teachers who may not be totally clear on the level of expectation for their students for a particular standard or concept. Joint planning and shared discussion help raise the level of student achievement as teachers look at student performance, examine student work, and discuss strategies to build student success. Once teacher teams have built some common assessments and agreed on and standardized exemplars and anchor papers for various tasks, teachers can confidently score student work knowing that the grade level has uniform standards and expectations in place.

Assessments are truly the circular link that tells us where to start our instruction, how much students have learned, and how much they still need to learn to demonstrate mastery. Since state tests and high-accountability measures are a reality in U.S. education, we must actively find ways to work more efficiently. We do that by clearly understanding what students are expected to do, sharing and collaborating with our peers, and helping students take responsibility for their own performance and improvement. With this change, we can truly deepen student thinking and become the wizard behind the curtain directing learning from behind the scenes.

Conclusion

While exposing students to a broad and comprehensive fact-based curriculum was valued in the 20th century, the rapid acceleration of knowledge during the last few decades means that just as the fabric of knowledge has changed, so too must our educational system change. Our focus must change from asking students to regurgitate facts and information to asking them to think deeply and apply higher-level processing skills to challenging tasks and curriculum. To be successful, students will need to analyze, synthesize, and evaluate the problems and issues facing them in an ever more complex world.

Whether we like it or not, the demand for high-stakes accountability is not going away anytime soon. In fact, it is likely that this pressure may even increase as researchers find ways to directly link a student's performance back to the actions of the teachers who have taught that individual. With this in mind, we must find as many ways as possible to be as efficient and effective as possible. Teachers must move out of the role of "keeper and dispenser of knowledge" and into the role of "diagnostician" who, through assessing student strengths and performance levels, can design the right blend of "coaching" to enable students to demonstrate high levels of excellence and successful performance.

Student learning is judged on how well students do on state evaluations. Therefore, we must thoroughly understand what students are expected to know and be able to do. By understanding the content standards and carefully analyzing performance, the effective teacher can provide a sequence of learning events individualized to each learner's needs. When we know the gap between what students bring to the task and what they still need to learn, we can create learning tasks that build and reinforce the type of higher-order thinking that students need to perform well on state content-area assessments.

In high-functioning schools where excellence thrives, the staff works together to share ideas, analyze concerns, and reflect on student learning. Teachers at the same grade level or in the same content area regularly collaborate to develop joint lesson plans, examine standards, and set expectations for student performance. Permeating the school is a culture of joint responsibility for the performance of all students and a "whatever it takes" attitude. By planning complex higher-order tasks and activities, monitoring performance expectations, and helping students self-analyze, the staff builds a community where deep thinking and learning thrive.

This book has been designed to help you go beyond the rote facts and memorization stage and to invite your students to truly apply the skills they are learning as independent and deep thinkers. We have closely examined many of the types of constructed-response items that your students might face in each content area. Your own scrutiny of your state's released materials and sample items can add to this body of information. The ideas and suggestions in this book are meant as springboards to stimulate your own thinking in each content area. The right instructional approaches are the ones that most closely match what it is that students are expected to be able to do.

We have also discussed how to build a supportive, collaborative school environment where the entire staff works to clarify expectations and set consistent, achievable performance measures. By harnessing the power of the many, we can make our own lives easier and magnify the impact of the one. When we prepare our students to do their best thinking on state and national assessments, we will also be preparing them to take their place as thoughtful, organized thinkers in the dynamic world of tomorrow.

Appendix A:
State Assessment Web Site Information

The following links may be helpful in locating information about your state assessment system and any released items that are available for you to view. While you should become extensively familiar with the standards, assessments, and any released items from your own state, feel free to peruse other states' sites, too, as many contain excellent lesson plan ideas for the various content areas as well as helpful sample assessments.

Please be aware that although this information is current at press time, links can and do frequently change. If these links no longer function, try going to the assessment section of your state Web site and looking for links to released items there, or search the state department site for the words "released items" to see if you can locate those materials.

Alabama: www.alsde.edu/html/sections/section_detail.asp?
    section=91&footer=sections
Alaska: www.eed.state.ak.us/Educators.html
Arizona: www.ade.az.gov/standards/aims/ReleaseItems/
Arkansas: http://arkedu.state.ar.us/actaap/student_
    assessment/student_assessment_p1.htm
California: www.cde.ca.gov/ta/tg/sr/resources.asp and
    www.score.k12.ca.us/
Colorado: www.cde.state.co.us/cdeassess/index_assess.html
Connecticut: www.state.ct.us/sde/DTL/curriculum/

Delaware: www.doe.k12.de.us/AAB/

Florida: www.fldoe.org/Default.asp?bhcp=1

Georgia: www.doe.k12.ga.us/curriculum/testing/crct_forms.asp

Hawaii: http://doe.k12.hi.us/viewpoints/assessment.htm

Idaho: www.boardofeducation.idaho.gov/saa/index.asp

Illinois: www.isbe.net/assessment

Indiana: www.doe.state.in.us/istep/

Iowa: www.education.uiowa.edu/itp/ited/ited_about.htm

Kansas: www.ksbe.state.ks.us/Welcome.html and http://education.
umkc.edu/kcrpdc/

Kentucky: www.education.ky.gov/KDE/Instructional+Resources/
Curriculum+Documents+and+Resources/Released+Test+Items/
default.htm and www.arsi.org/curriculum.asp?collab=

Louisiana: www.doe.state.la.us/lde/index.html

Maine: www.maptasks.org/

Maryland: http://mdk12.org/mspp/index.html

Massachusetts: www.doe.mass.edu/mcas/testitems.html

Michigan: www.michigan.gov/mde/0,1607,7-140-22709_31168_
31355---,00.html

Minnesota: http://education.state.mn.us/mde/Accountability_
Programs/Assessment_and_Testing/Assessments/MCA_II/
MCA_II_Item_Samplers/index.html

Mississippi: www.mde.k12.ms.us/acad/osa/gltpprac.html

Missouri: http://dese.mo.gov/divimprove/assess/ and
www.successlink.org/

Montana: www.opi.state.mt.us/Assessment/Phase2.html

Nebraska: www.nde.state.ne.us/stars/pdf/STARSbooklet.pdf

Nevada: www.doe.nv.gov/statetesting/critreftests.html

New Hampshire: www.ed.state.nh.us/education/doe/
organization/curriculum/Assessment.htm

New Jersey: www.state.nj.us/njded/assessment/ and www.
njpep.org

New Mexico: www.ped.state.nm.us/div/ais/assess/

New York: www.emsc.nysed.gov/osa/ and http://nysut.org/
standards

North Carolina: www.ncpublicschools.org/accountability/
    testing/
North Dakota: www.dpi.state.nd.us/standard/asments/index.shtm
Ohio: www.ode.state.oh.us/proficiency/
Oklahoma: http://title3.sde.state.ok.us/studentassessment/
    testingmaterials.htm
Oregon: www.ode.state.or.us/search/results/?id=169
Pennsylvania: www.pde.state.pa.us/a_and_t/site/default.asp
Rhode Island: www.ridoe.net/standards/default.htm,
    www.ride.ri.gov/learningpt/exampledefinitions/, and
    www.necompact.org/ea/gle_support/NECAP_2005.asp
South Carolina: http://ed.sc.gov/topics/assessment/
South Dakota: http://doe.sd.gov/octa/assessment/
Tennessee: http://state.tn.us/education/assessment/
Texas: www.tea.state.tx.us/student.assessment
Utah: www.usoe.k12.ut.us/eval/Menu.asp
Vermont: www.state.vt.us/educ/new/html/pgm_assessment.
    html
Virginia: http://education.jlab.org/solquiz/index.html
Washington: www.k12.wa.us/assessment/WASL
West Virginia: http://osa.k12.wv.us/
Wisconsin: http://dpi.wi.gov/oea/assessmt.html
Wyoming: www.k12.wy.us/sa.asp

Other Sources of Information on Assessment

Educator's Reference Desk: www.eduref.org/
Kathy Schrock's Webguide to Assessments for Teachers:
    http://school.discovery.com/schrockguide/assess.html
National Assessment of Educational Progress:
    http://nces.ed.gov/nationsreportcard/ITMRLS/ITMRLS.htm
TIMMS site on math and science: http://nces.ed.gov/timss/ and
    http://ustimss.msu.edu/

Appendix B:
Virtual Field Trip, Activity,
and Rubric Web Sites

The Internet is filled with wonderful resources to help students explore learning in unique and original ways. Here are some that I particularly like. Although Web sites often change content or even disappear altogether, the following sites provide good information for virtual field trips and activities that you can use to design solid exploratory units. Please preview all sites for age and content appropriateness before you invite students to visit them.

Language Arts

Caribbean Authors on the Web: Site promoting works of Caribbean authors, including slave narratives, poems, and other facts about life in the islands. Maintained by the University of Miami. http://scholar.library.miami.edu/anthurium/home.htm.

Poe: Familiarize yourself with the mysterious life and works of Edgar Allan Poe. Great interactive site. http://knowingpoe.thinkport. org/default_flash.asp

Threads of Reading: Teacher and author resource links for reading and language arts. www.threadsofreading.com

Science

Enviromysteries: Site that discusses the links between rising health problems such as asthma, cancer, and new viruses and their

relationship to the environment. http://enviromysteries.
thinkport.org/

Exploratorium: Web site of the San Francisco Exploratorium. Many
fun projects and things to learn at this site. www.exploratorium.
edu/

Jason Project: Each year the Jason Project explores a new aspect of
the scientific world. Students can interact with real scientists.
www.jasonproject.org/

Millennium Seed Bank Project: Site from the Royal Botanic Gardens
about seeds and flowering plants. Contains a Seed Information
Database where visitors can classify their own seeds. www.
rbgkew.org.uk/msbp/

Ocean Science Institute: Learn about ocean projects, sharks, and
fishery projects. Site includes images, videos, and audio
programs on all aspects of marine life and preservation.
www.pewoceanscience.org

Perfect Disaster: A Discovery Channel site to learn about typhoons,
thunderstorms, and hurricanes. Great hands-on experiences!
http://dsc.discovery.com

Plastic Fork Diaries: Site for middle school students on eating, nutri-
tion, and performance. Examining how what we eat affects who
we are. www.plasticforkdiaries.com/index_flash.cfm

Project Wise: Interactive site for students in grades 4–12 to use simulations, visualizations, and other materials for inquiry-based science study. Registration for students and teachers is free.
http://wise.berkeley.edu/welcome.php

Thinkport: Hands-on learning with virtual field trips of all types.
www.thinkport.org/classroom/trips.tp

Wildlife Conservation Society: Site from the Wildlife Conservation
Society with great links to conservation projects around the
world, as well as links to the New York Aquarium and several
New York zoos. www.wcs.org/

Wildlife Research Center: Patuxent Wildlife Research Center in Maryland provides this site about wildlife and natural resources in the
Northeast. Spotlight section contains a frog call quiz and video
clips of wildlife. Site has an area where students can ask questions of resident biologists. www.pwrc.usgs.gov/

Social Studies

American History Collection: Site containing over 100 historical documents relating to U.S. history from 1400 to the present. Includes letters, essays, charters, speeches, journals, inaugural addresses, and more. http://odur.let.rug.nl/~usa/usa.htm

American Memories: Library of Congress National Digital Library containing over 40 collections of historical photos, maps, documents, letters, speeches, recordings, videos, and more. http://memory.loc.gov/ammem/

American South: Archive from the University of North Carolina at Chapel Hill with primary source slavery narratives and first-person narratives about life in the South. Also contains a digitized library of Southern literature. http://metalab.unc.edu/docsouth/

Ancient World Web: Searchable site indexing thousands of sites on ancient world history. www.julen.net/ancient/

Economic History Services: Good information on comparing economic factors from the past to the present. See more information on this site under the same heading in the math category. http://eh.net

Henry Ford Museum: Site from the Henry Ford Museum featuring an "Explore and Learn" area that contains a number of exhibits such as a tour of the bus that carried Rosa Parks. Innovators area includes information about Thomas Edison, R. Buckminster Fuller, and others. http://hfmgv.org/

Hirshhorn Smithsonian Museum: Site features the work of Hiroshi Sugimoto from 1976 to the present. Photos available include architectural designs as well as many 16th-century portraits of Henry VIII and his wives. www.hirshhorn.si.edu/sugimoto

History Net: Collection of materials for U.S. and world history through eyewitness accounts, interviews, photos, and other primary and secondary sources. www.thehistorynet.com

Jefferson Davis Papers: Writings and documents from Jefferson Davis, president of the Confederacy, providing background on his life and family. http://jeffersondavis.rice.edu

Labyrinth: Collection of medieval resources including poetry and prose, information about medieval cultures, and teaching resources. www.georgetown.edu/labyrinth/labyrinth-home.html

Library of Congress: Tremendous resources for teachers and students for primary documents in American history. Contains lots of lesson plans and ideas for teachers. www.loc.gov/teachers/

Lincoln Virtual Library: Library of Congress presentation on Lincoln. Includes the Emancipation Proclamation and information on the president's assassination. Great collection of online resources. http://memory.loc.gov/ammem/alhtml/alhome.html

National Archives: Great resource with tons of documents to use with students, including excellent lesson plans and tips for educators. Contains documents such as the Declaration of Independence, the Constitution, the Bill of Rights, and even a copy of the arrest record for Rosa Parks. Exhibit Hall contains primary sources on the Lincoln assassination and World War II propaganda posters. www.archives.gov/education/

New Deal Network: Site contains primary source information related to the Depression and the New Deal era. Includes letters, photos, documents, speeches, posters, and political cartoons from the era. http://newdeal.feri.org/

Sacred Destinations: A great collection containing information on more than 1,500 sacred sites around the world. Browse category themes such as Shinto shrines, Buddhist temples, Jewish museums, and so forth. Includes lots of pictures of each place as well. www.sacred-destinations.com

San Francisco Historical Photo Collection: Historical photography collection of San Francisco including the infamous earthquake of 1906. Site contains over 250,000 photos, including thematic collections. http://sfpl.lib.ca.us/librarylocations/sfhistory/sfphoto.htm

Song of America: Library of Congress project on the history of music in America. Lots of concert presentations on historical song in the United States. http://lcweb2.loc.gov/cocoon/ihas/html/songofamerica/songofamerica.html

Time Cover Collection at the National Portrait Gallery: The National Portrait Gallery at the Smithsonian presents a collection of over 2,000 of the portraits from the covers of *Time* magazine with biographical sketches and some video, such as Martin Luther King's "I Have a Dream" speech. Includes organization by themes. www.time.com/time/coversearch

Tower of London Virtual Tour: Explore the inside of the Tower of London and English history with this great visual tour. www.toweroflondontour.com/

Vincent Voice Library: Site features primary source sound recordings. Includes speech clips from many U.S. presidents and other famous people. www.lib.msu.edu/vincent/

Virtual Vaudeville: Help students understand the era of vaudeville with this three-dimensional simulation site. www.virtualvaudeville.com

Math

Economic History Services: Good information on economics along with a "How much is that?" service where visitors can find historical prices for goods and services, interest rates, wage rates, and inflation rates. Questions can also be answered about economic factors such as "Is deflation bad for the economy?" Good for developing units comparing costs today with costs of previous eras. http://eh.net

Illuminations: Links from the National Council of Teachers of Mathematics that connect to all five strands of the standards. Outstanding resource of Web sites of every type. http://illuminations. nctm.org/Weblinks.aspx

Math Hotlist of Virtual Field Trip Sites: A collection of interesting sites that relate to learning math. www.kn.pacbell.com/wired/fil/ pages/listvirtualgr.html

Sense and Dollars: Fun site about the value of money. Learn about how credit cards work, how long it will take to earn enough money for a new MP3 player, or what it will cost to go to the prom. Play money games. Great interactive site with solid learning embedded in the process. http://senseanddollars. thinkport.org/

Villainy, Inc.: Designed for middle school math students. Features problem solving à la James Bond adventure. Students foil the plans of the evil Dr. Wick in an animated mission using critical thinking and math calculation. http://villainyinc.thinkport.org/

Virtual Field Trips in Math: A collection of Web resources that help students improve their understandings of math. http://mathforum.org/library/resource_types/net/

Additional Web Resources for All Content Areas and Hands-On, Minds-On Learning

Apple Learning Interchange: Apple's site for teachers and students featuring lesson plans, student work, assessment, virtual field trips, and much more. http://edcommunity.apple.com/ali/

Edutopia: Project-Based Learning: The George Lucas Educational Foundation site dedicated to helping teachers learn about project-based learning for grades K–12. Excellent source of videos, lesson plans, assessments, and other ideas to help teachers move instruction to higher and more effective levels. www.edutopia.org/foundation/topics.php

Eisenhower National Clearinghouse for Math and Science Education: Site has curriculum and professional development resources. www.goenc.com

Innovation Odyssey: Intel's site for Innovation Odyssey and many other exciting ways to use technology to enhance content learning and teaching effectiveness. www.intel.com/education/sections/section1/index.htm

Kathy Schrock's Webguide: Great activities in all content areas on the Web. http://school.discovery.com/schrockguide/index.html

Learning about Rubrics: Helpful site that explains why teachers should use rubrics in the classroom and provides guidance on how to develop them. http://learnweb.harvard.edu/alps/thinking/docs/rubricar.htm

Math Instruction Resources: A wealth of hands-on activities for the middle school math teacher. A great source of lesson plan ideas. http://fcit.usf.edu/FCAT8m/resource/default.htm

Microsoft Virtual Classroom Tours: Site offers creative activities for students of all grade levels as well as good information for teachers on effective hands-on teaching practices. www.microsoft.com/education/InTeachersVCT.mspx

Online Resource Collection: Site includes teacher resources, Web sites, and information for all content areas, including science, social studies, the arts, health/physical education, foreign languages, and literature. http://fcit.usf.edy/fcat8r/files/win/s6/61020c.htm

Online Virtual Fieldtrips: A collection of online virtual field trip resources for all content areas. www.thinkport.org/Classroom/trips.tp

Virtual Field Trip Links: Links to many outstanding virtual field trips for all content areas. www.nvo.com/ecnewletter/virtualfield-trips/

Rubric Sources

There are many outstanding resources for rubrics on the Internet. Here are some excellent ones to get you started.

www.tnellen.com/cybereng/38/html#rubrics

http://school.discovery.com/schrockguide/assess.html

http://techlearning.com/db_area/archives/WCE/archives/valguid.html

http://pareonline.net/getvn.asp?v=7&n=25

www.teach-nology.com/web_tools/rubrics

www.rubrics.com

http://rubistar.4teachers.org/index.php

www.rubrics4teachers.com/

http://school.discovery.com/schrockguide/assess.html

www.kenton.k12.ky.us/tr/rubrics.html

www.webenglishteacher.com/rubrics.html

www.uwstout.edu/soe/profdev/rubrics.shtml

www.sdcoe.k12.ca.us/score/actbank/trubrics.htm

www.tcet.unt.edu/START/instruct/general/rubrics.htm

http://webquest.sdsu.edu/rubrics/weblessons.htm

www.techtrekers.com/rubrics.html

References

Allen, D. (Ed.). (1998). *Assessing student learning: From grading to understanding.* New York: Teachers College Press.

Allen, D., & Blythe, T. (2003). *A facilitator's book of questions: Resources for looking together at student and teacher work.* New York: Teachers College Press.

Annenberg Institute for School Reform. (1997). *Looking at student work: A window into the classroom.* VIDEO.

Ball, D. L. (2006). Research on teaching mathematics: Making subject matter knowledge part of the equation. Available: http://ncrtl.msu.edu/http/ rreports/html/pdf/rr882.pdf. Unpublished paper to appear in J. Brophy (Ed.), *Advances in research on teaching: Vol. 2. Teachers, subject matter knowledge and classroom instruction.* Greenwich, CT: JAI Press.

Blythe, T., Allen, D., & Powell, B. (1999). *Looking together at student work.* New York: Teachers College Press.

Fox, M.(1993). *Radical reflections.* San Diego, CA: Harcourt Brace.

Graham, B., & Fahey, K. (1999, March). School leaders look at student work. *Educational Leadership, 56*(6), 25–27.

Joyce, B., & Showers, B. (2002). *Student achievement through staff development* (3rd ed.). Alexandria, VA: Association for Supervision and Curriculum Development.

Keene, E., & Zimmerman, S. (1997). *Mosaic of thought.* Portsmouth, NH: Heinemann.

Langer, G. M., Colton, A. B., & Goff, L. S. (2003). *Collaborative analysis of student work: Improving teaching and learning.* Alexandria, VA: Association for Supervision and Curriculum Development.

Lockhead, J., & Clement, J. (Eds.). (1979). *Cognitive process instruction: Research on teaching thinking skills.* Philadelphia: Franklin Institute.

Marzano, R. J., & Pickering, D. J. (2005). *Building active vocabulary.* Alexandria, VA: Association for Supervision and Curriculum Development.

Marzano, R. J., Pickering, D. J., & Pollock, J. E. (2001). *Classroom instruction that works.* Alexandria, VA: Association for Supervision and Curriculum Development.

Metzenberg, S. (n.d.). Improving state science assessments. Retrieved July 10, 2007 from http://escience.ws/stm/StateScienceAssess.pdf.

Montgomery County Public Schools. (2002). *HAS rubric for constructed-response items: Science.* Rockville, MD: Author. Available: www.mcps.k12.md.us/ curriculum/science/forms/rubrictable.pdf.

Northwest Regional Education Laboratory. (2002). *Implementing project-based instruction: Essentials for structuring projects effectively.* Portland, OR: Author. Available: www.nwrel.org/request/2002aug/implementing.html.

Ripple, R., & Drinkwater, D. (1982). Transfer of learning. In M. C. Alkin (Ed.), *Encyclopedia of educational research* (Vol. 4, pp. 1947–1953). New York: Macmillan.

Roth, K., Druker, S., Garnier, H., Lemmens, M., Chen, C., Kawanaka, T., et al. (2006). *Teaching science in five countries: Results from the TIMSS 1999 Video Study (NCES 2006-011).* Washington, DC: National Center for Education Statistics. Available: http://nces.ed.gov/times.

Roth, K., & Garnier, H. (2007). What science teaching looks like: An international perspective. *Educational Leadership, 64*(4), 16–23.

Schafersman, S. D. (1991). *An introduction to critical thinking.* Available: www.freeinquiry.com/critical-thinking.html.

Tankersley, K. (2003). *Threads of reading: Strategies for literacy development.* Alexandria, VA: Association for Supervision and Curriculum Development.

Tankersley, K. (2005). *Literacy strategies for grades 4–12: Reinforcing the threads of reading.* Alexandria, VA: Association for Supervision and Curriculum Development.

U.S. Department of Labor. (2007). Fastest growing occupations covered in the 2006–07 Occupational Outlook Handbook, 2004–14. Retrieved March 1, 2007, from www.bls.gov/newsrelease/ooh.t01.htm.

Wiggins, G., & McTighe, J. (1998). *Understanding by design.* Alexandria, VA: Association for Supervision and Curriculum Development.

Wilson, M. R., & Bertenthal, M. W. (Eds.). (2005). *Systems for state science assessment.* Washington, DC: National Academies Press.

Wormeli, R. (2004). *Summarization in any subject: 50 techniques to improve student learning.* Alexandria, VA: Association for Supervision and Curriculum Development.

Young, B. (1996). *Free stuff for science buffs.* Scottsdale, AZ: Coriolis Group Books.

Index

Note: page numbers followed by *f* refer to figures

About the Author

Karen Tankersley, a 28-year veteran of public school service, resides in Phoenix, Arizona. Karen left public service in May 2004 and currently works with school districts across the United States on school improvement and professional development activities. A resident of Arizona since her early teen years, Karen likes the desert and the Southwest lifestyle. She enjoys travel, swimming, reading, and spending time with her two young granddaughters.

Originally a linguist with a Bachelor of Arts degree in French and minors in German and English, Karen spent several years living in Europe and serving as a translator of German documents. She has an extensive background in language and language acquisition issues, holds a Master of Arts in Reading and a Doctor of Philosophy in Educational Leadership and Policy Studies from Arizona State University.

Karen has teaching experience at all grades from 2 to 12 and also at the university level. In her early career, she spent 10 years in various roles as a classroom teacher, foreign language teacher, reading specialist, and teacher of the gifted and talented. She served for 13 years as a principal in schools recognized nationally for their outstanding achievement and high academic performance. Karen spent five years at the district office level where she served at the superintendent level and oversaw the Educational Services and Assessment efforts of a growing, suburban school district. She currently is employed as a clinical professor at Arizona State University, West Campus, in Phoenix.

Karen enjoys writing and has published articles in several educational journals including *Educational Leadership*. She is the author of *The Threads of Reading: Strategies for Literacy Development* (ASCD, 2003) and *Literacy Strategies for Grades 4–12: Reinforcing the Threads of Reading* (ASCD, 2005) on effective strategies for reading instruction. Karen's Web site, www.threadsofreading.com, provides a wealth of valuable information on effective reading instruction for educators. Karen can be reached at kt@threadsofreading.com.

Related ASCD Resources: Assessment

At the time of publication, the following ASCD resources were available (ASCD stock numbers appear in parentheses). For up-to-date information about ASCD resources, go to www.ascd.org.

Multimedia

Formative Assessment Strategies for Every Classroom—An ASCD Action Tool (#707010)

Networks

Visit the ASCD Web site (www.ascd.org) and search for "networks" for information about professional educators who have formed groups around topics like "Assessment for Learning" and "Teaching Thinking." Look in the "Network Directory" for current facilitators' addresses and phone numbers.

Online Courses

Exemplary Assessment: Measurement That's Useful by Jenny Smith

Print Products

Educational Leadership (February 2003): Using Data to Improve Student Achievement (#103031)

Test Better, Teach Better: The Instructional Role of Assessment by W. James Popham (#102088)

The Truth About Testing: An Educator's Call to Action by W. James Popham (#101030)

Videotapes

Balanced Assessment: Improving Student Achievement and Standardized Test Results Bundle (three-tape video set; one DVD; two facilitator's guides) (#704451)

How to Prepare Students for Standardized Tests (#401014)

Redesigning Assessments (three-tape series with three facilitator's guides) (#614237)

Using Classroom Assessment to Guide Instruction (three-tape series with facilitator's guide) (#402286)

Using Standards, Tape 2: Improving Curriculum and Assessment (#400264)

For more information: send e-mail to member@ascd.org; call 1-800-933-2723 or 703-578-9600, press 2; send a fax to 703-575-5400; or write to Information Services, ASCD, 1703 N. Beauregard St., Alexandria, VA 22311-1714 USA.

TESTS
that TEACH